ISRAEL ALIVE AGAIN

ISRAEL ALIVE AGAIN

A Commentary on the Books of

Ezra and Nehemiah

FREDRICK CARLSON HOLMGREN

WM. B. EERDMANS PUBL. CO., GRAND RAPIDS

THE HANDSEL PRESS LTD, EDINBURGH

Copyright © 1987 by Wm. B. Eerdmans Publishing Company
First published 1987 by William B. Eerdmans Publishing Company,
255 Jefferson Ave. S.E., Grand Rapids, Michigan 49503
and
The Handsel Press Limited
33 Montgomery Street, Edinburgh EH7 5JX

Library of Congress Cataloging-in-Publication Data

Holmgren, Fredrick Carlson, 1926-
Israel alive again.

(International theological commentary)
Bibliography: p. 159
1. Bible. O.T. Ezra — Commentaries. 2. Bible.
O.T. Nehemiah — Commentaries. I. Title. II. Series.
BS1355.3.H65   1987   222'.707   87-5283

ISBN 0-8028-0259-1

Handsel edition 905312 67 8

CONTENTS

Editors' Preface	viii
Author's Preface	xii
Introduction	xiii
Abbreviations	xviii

THE BOOK OF EZRA

Israel Alive Again (1:1-11)	3
The Exiles Return to the Land (2:1-70)	14
Beginning Again (3:1-13)	20
Effective Opposition (4:1-24)	28
The Rebuilding of the Temple (5:1-17)	36
The Temple Built: Divine-Human Partnership (6:1-22)	44
Ezra Arrives with Torah (7:1-28)	55
A New Exodus (8:1-36)	65
Intermarriage (9:1-15)	71
Prayer, Firm Action, and Repentance (10:1-44)	80

THE BOOK OF NEHEMIAH

Jerusalem in Ruins (1:1-11)	89
From Palace Life to Jerusalem's Ruins (2:1-20)	95
Working Together to Rebuild the Wall (3:1-32)	102
With Hard Work, Weapons, and the Help of God (4:1-23)	105
Internal Problems (5:1-19)	109
Success in Sight but Still Opposition (6:1-19)	115
These Are the Pioneers (7:1-73a)	120

Ezra Reads the Torah (7:73b – 8:18)   122

Repentance and Confession (9:1-37)   129

A Firm Covenant (9:38 – 10:39)   136

The People of Jerusalem and Judah (11:1-36)   141

Priests and Levites and the Dedication of the Wall (12:1-47)   144

Either — Or (13:1-31)   148

Bibliography of Works Cited   159

With Memory of
Clare and Gustaf Carlson
&
Freda and Charles Holmgren

EDITORS' PREFACE

The Old Testament alive in the Church: this is the goal of the *International Theological Commentary*. Arising out of changing, unsettled times, this Scripture speaks with an authentic voice to our own troubled world. It witnesses to God's ongoing purpose and to his caring presence in the universe without ignoring those experiences of life that cause one to question his existence and love. This commentary series is written by front-rank scholars who treasure the life of faith.

Addressed to ministers and Christian educators, the *International Theological Commentary* moves beyond the usual critical-historical approach to the Bible and offers a *theological* interpretation of the Hebrew text. Thus, engaging larger textual units of the biblical writings, the authors of these volumes assist the reader in the appreciation of the theology underlying the text as well as its place in the thought of the Hebrew Scriptures. But more, since the Bible is the book of the believing community, its text has acquired ever more meaning through an ongoing interpretation. This growth of interpretation may be found both within the Bible itself and in the continuing scholarship of the Church.

Contributors to the *International Theological Commentary* are Christians—persons who affirm the witness of the New Testament concerning Jesus Christ. For Christians, the Bible is *one* scripture containing the Old and New Testaments. For this reason, a commentary on the Old Testament may not ignore the second part of the canon, namely, the New Testament.

Since its beginning, the Church has recognized a special relationship between the two Testaments. But the precise character of this bond has been difficult to define. The diversity of views represented in these publications makes us aware that the Church is not of one mind in expressing the "how" of this relationship. The authors of this series share a developing consensus that any serious explanation of the Old Testament's relationship to the New will uphold the integrity of the Old Testament. Even though

Christianity is rooted in the soil of the Hebrew Scriptures, the biblical interpreter must take care lest he "christianize" these Scriptures.

Authors writing in this commentary series will, no doubt, hold various views concerning *how* the Old Testament relates to the New. No attempt has been made to dictate one viewpoint in this matter. With the whole Church, we are convinced that the relationship between the two Testaments is real and substantial. But we recognize also the diversity of opinions among Christian scholars when they attempt to articulate fully the nature of this relationship.

In addition to the Christian Church, there exists another people for whom the Old Testament is important, namely, the Jewish community. Both Jews and Christians claim the Hebrew Bible as Scripture. Jews believe that the basic teachings of this Scripture point toward, and are developed by, the Talmud, which assumed its present form about 500 C.E. On the other hand, Christians hold that the Old Testament finds its fulfillment in the New Testament. The Hebrew Bible, therefore, belongs to both the Church and the Synagogue.

Recent studies have demonstrated how profoundly early Christianity reflects a Jewish character. This fact is not surprising because the Christian movement arose out of the context of first-century Judaism. Further, Jesus himself was Jewish, as were the first Christians. It is to be expected, therefore, that Jewish and Christian interpretations of the Hebrew Bible will reveal similarities *and* disparities. Such is the case. The authors of the *International Theological Commentary* will refer to the various Jewish traditions that they consider important for an appreciation of the Old Testament text. Such references will enrich our understanding of certain biblical passages and, as an extra gift, offer us insight into the relationship of Judaism to early Christianity.

An important second aspect of the present series is its *international* character. In the past, Western church leaders were considered to be *the* leaders of the Church — at least by those living in the West! The theology and biblical exegesis done by these scholars dominated the thinking of the Church. Most commentaries were produced in the Western world and reflected the lifestyle, needs, and thoughts of its civilization. But the Christian Church is a worldwide community. People who belong to the universal Church reflect differing thoughts, needs, and lifestyles.

Today the fastest growing churches in the world are to be found, not in the West, but in Africa, Indonesia, South America,

Korea, Taiwan, and elsewhere. By the end of the century, Christians in these areas will outnumber those who live in the West. In our age, especially, a commentary on the Bible must transcend the parochialism of Western civilization and be sensitive to issues that are the special problems of persons who live outside the "Christian" West, issues such as race relations, personal survival and fulfillment, liberation, revolution, famine, tyranny, disease, war, the poor, religion and state. Inspired by God, the authors of the Old Testament knew what life is like on the edge of existence. They addressed themselves to everyday people who often faced more than everyday problems. Refusing to limit God to the "spiritual," they portrayed him as one who heard and knew the cries of people in pain (see Exod. 3:7-8). The contributors to the *International Theological Commentary* are persons who prize the writings of these biblical authors as a word of life to our world today. They read the Hebrew Scriptures in the contexts of ancient Israel and our modern day.

The scholars selected as contributors underscore the international aspect of the Commentary. Representing very different geographical, ideological, and ecclesiastical backgrounds, they come from over seventeen countries. Besides scholars from such traditional countries as England, Scotland, France, Italy, Switzerland, Canada, New Zealand, Australia, South Africa, and the United States, contributors from the following places are included: Israel, Indonesia, India, Thailand, Singapore, Taiwan, and countries of Eastern Europe. Such diversity makes for richness of thought. Christian scholars living in Buddhist, Muslim, or Socialist lands may be able to offer the World Church insights into the biblical message — insights to which the scholarship of the West could be blind.

The proclamation of the biblical message is the focal concern of the *International Theological Commentary*. Generally speaking, the authors of these commentaries value the historical-critical studies of past scholars, but they are convinced that these studies by themselves are not enough. The Bible is more than an object of critical study; it is the revelation of God. In the written Word, God has disclosed himself and his will to humankind. Our authors see themselves as servants of the Word which, when rightly received, brings *shalom* to both the individual and the community.

Those who preserve traditions unchanged often, through such rigidity, contribute to the dissolution of a movement that once nurtured an earlier generation. But change that fails to treasure the *core* of a tradition betrays that tradition and effectively spells its end. Life is often lived between these two alternatives. Such was the situation for those exiles who returned to the land in the 6th and 5th centuries B.C.E.

The books of Ezra and Nehemiah provide insight into the issues of that day—and they are issues not far removed from some basic questions that we strive to answer today. For example, with the people of this earlier time we share the following concerns: (1) To what extent is the *life* of faith tied to earlier forms? For them the question concerned the rebuilding of the temple and the city walls. For us the precise question may be different but the issue is the same. (2) The God of Patriarchs and Prophets was the God who intervened in history. What kind of help can we expect from God? How much does the outcome of life depend on our effort and wisdom? (3) Should "common sense" ever take precedence over "theology"? (4) How does a community prevent grace from becoming "cheap" grace? (5) How open should the community of faith be? When should it say yes, when no? (6) What kind of future do we wish for our children? These and other questions make us aware that the world of Ezra and Nehemiah is our world. These books are rich sources for the minister as he or she attempts to provide guidance to present-day congregations.

This commentary is concerned to interpret Ezra-Nehemiah in the context of the Hebrew Bible, but because both the Synagogue and the Church view these writings as Scripture, comments on the text sometimes refer to the New Testament and the Talmud. Awareness of these two communities has also led to the use of the following abbreviations: B.C.E. (Before the Common Era) and C.E. (the Common Era). This commentary on Ezra-Nehemiah is the contribution of a Christian scholar, but we hope at some points it may contain authentic words for Jews as well as for Christians.

—George A. F. Knight
—Fredrick Carlson Holmgren

AUTHOR'S PREFACE

With other volumes in this series, the present one addresses itself to ministers and focuses on the *theological* aspect of the biblical text. I have benefited significantly from the work of recent commentators and am pleased to acknowledge that my contribution is the richer because of the gifts of others.

My association with G. A. F. Knight, Co-Editor of the *International Theological Commentary,* has been a delightful one. For years he has dreamed of a commentary series that would focus on the theological implications of the biblical text; I am happy to be a part of his dream-come-true! Further, I am thankful to Mr. Marlin Van Elderen, former Editor-in-Chief at William B. Eerdmans Publishing Company, for inviting me to be a co-editor of this series, and I am happy now to be working with Mr. Jon Pott, who is the present Editor-in-Chief.

I am also grateful to several friends who have taken a special interest in my work: the Reverend Glenn Palmberg, a former colleague, and his wife, Sharon, who have given continuing support for research and writing; Mr. James Theorell, whose grant assisted me in my beginning research on postexilic Judaism; the Reverend Timothy Sporrong, who read the manuscript and made a number of helpful suggestions. Finally, my life with Betty has made me more fully aware of how closely tied are the words "separate" and "together."

Chicago
Fredrick Carlson Holmgren
July 1986

INTRODUCTION

AUTHOR AND DATE

The books of Ezra and Nehemiah, considered originally to be one book in the Jewish tradition, assumed their present form ca. 300 B.C.E. Many present-day scholars assert that the anonymous author of 1-2 Chronicles (called the Chronicler) was responsible for the writing of these two books. But Sarah Japhet ("The Supposed Common Authorship of Chronicles and Ezra-Nehemiah Investigated Anew," *VT* 18 [1968]: 330-71) and others have challenged this view, believing that Ezra-Nehemiah is the work of another author. In our commentary we lean to the latter view and have simply referred to the one responsible for the present form of Ezra and Nehemiah as the "author" or "editor."

CHARACTER AND FOCUS

Living between 400 and 300 B.C.E. (see H. G. M. Williamson, *Ezra, Nehemiah,* xxxvi), the author tells the story of the return of the Jewish exiles to the land of Israel after having spent many years of exile in Babylon. He begins "his-story" with the decree of Cyrus (539 B.C.E.), which allowed Jews and other captive peoples to return to their homelands. His main theme is: Israel is alive again — raised from the death of the Exile (cf. Ezek. 37:1-14). The land that was left desolate by the Babylonian army in 587 B.C.E. is peopled once again with Jews faithful to the Torah who give themselves to the arduous task of rebuilding the temple (Ezra) and the walls about Jerusalem (Nehemiah). Both Ezra and Nehemiah speak of the activity of these Jews, who, committed to the ancient Sinai (Mosaic) traditions, institute radical measures to preserve these old, lifegiving values for their children (cf., e.g., Ezra 10; Neh. 9:38 – 10:39; 12:1-47). The people known as "Israel" before the Exile are now identified as "Jews." The English term "Jew" comes from the Hebrew word *yehudi,* that is, Judahite (Esth. 2:5; cf. the plural form in Neh. 1:2).

The years covered by these two books (ca. 538-400 B.C.E.) were difficult years for the struggling community. Not only were their chosen goals themselves hard to reach, but dissension from within and determined opposition from without multiplied the difficulty of their task. Nevertheless, their leaders were optimistic; they believed that they had a future because God was working *with them* to accomplish his purpose in their period of history. The book of Daniel, which follows Ezra and Nehemiah in the Jewish canon, has a very different emphasis: Hope for the future is grounded almost entirely in God alone.

To speak further about this optimistic character of Ezra and Nehemiah, some additional comment about the canonical shape of the Hebrew Bible is needed. The Jewish canon differs significantly from the Christian canon; whereas the latter canon of the Hebrew Bible ends with the book of Malachi, the Jewish canon ends with 2 Chronicles. For Christians, Malachi (ending with the fervent hope for the day of the LORD) appears to be longing for some special divine action to take place. The Christian Church has frequently understood Malachi's expectation of the "day of the LORD" to represent the whole OT's hope for the coming of Jesus Christ (Mark 9:12; cf. 1:2). Because in Christian circles the OT ended with Malachi, this interpretation had a special attraction for the Church. But, as we have said, in the Jewish canon the Hebrew Bible ends not with Malachi but with Ezra, Nehemiah, and 1-2 Chronicles. The final verses of 2 Chronicles (36:22-23) contain the announcement that Yahweh *has* intervened on behalf of the Jews in exile. In the midst of their suffering, he is creating a future for them.

The manner of this intervention is astonishing; Yahweh has chosen Cyrus, king of Persia, to be the one who will enable the exiles to return home and rebuild the temple. Thus Chronicles does not end with a look to the distant future but with the affirmation that deliverance and restoration are happening now. It is this story that the books of Ezra and Nehemiah preserve for us. The point of our comments above is this: the last three books of the Jewish canon are optimistic about the present and near future even though the times are difficult.

EZRA AND NEHEMIAH

Although a number of persons emerged as leaders in this pioneer community, the principal leaders among the returnees were Ezra and Nehemiah. We do not know all that much about them, however, because the character of these books (as we have intimated) is not that of an exact history. One could say that it is a religious history, since Ezra and Nehemiah witness — testify — to God working with faithful Jews to reestablish the covenant community in the land. The writer's concern is not to provide information about this period of history. This is not to say that these books lack a historical base; rather it means that historical details are mentioned only as they serve to fill out this witness. As we will see in the Commentary, the reader is often left in the dark with regard to dates, events, and relationships. For example, the text of Ezra leaves us with questions about the accomplishments of Sheshbazzar and his relationship to Zerubbabel.

Further, to the distress of scholars, we have little firm information concerning the relationship of Ezra to Nehemiah; in fact, we are not certain which one arrived first in the community of the returnees. The traditional view is that Ezra preceded Nehemiah, coming from Babylon ca. 458 B.C.E. (see Ezra 7:8). According to this view, Nehemiah arrived some thirteen years later, in 445 B.C.E. Many modern interpreters question this chronology and affirm on the basis of forceful arguments that Nehemiah preceded Ezra in the leadership of the community of returned exiles. These scholars would place Ezra's arrival in the year 398, or possibly in 428. The discussion is complicated; the reader who is interested in this matter may consult other commentaries listed in the bibliography (see, e.g., Derek Kidner, *Ezra and Nehemiah*, 146-58; and D. J. A. Clines, *Ezra, Nehemiah, Esther*, 14-24).

Although the issue of the chronological relationship of these two leaders is important in itself, the solution of this problem is not critical to the chief concern of this commentary, which is: a theological probe of the text of Ezra and Nehemiah. For this reason, we simply note (for the most part) the ambiguity of the relationship between Ezra and Nehemiah and comment on the text as it has been handed down to us in the canon.

EZRA IN LATER LITERATURE

In the person of Ezra, "a scribe skilled in the law of Moses" (Ezra 7:6), we are able to see the emergence of the core of what is now called Rabbinic Judaism. With him emerges a firm emphasis on the study of the Law (Torah) — a written tradition which needed interpretation. Jacob Agus observes (*The Evolution of Jewish Thought*, 48):

> While the Deuteronomist urges the Israelites to consult prophets in the event of doubt, Ezra and his contemporaries seek guidance in the diligent study of the written documents. The living but temperamental and unpredictable instrument of the Word of God that the prophet had been was now replaced by the rigid but certain book. . . . Now that the Torah of Moses was standardized, it appeared that the prophet could not controvert any of its numerous precepts, which in turn could be stretched by interpretation to cover almost every contingency in life.

Ezra is often called "the Father of Judaism," a title that is justified by his work in the 5th century B.C.E. Still today most Jews believe that the book of Ezra is of "major significance" and should be *"studied by Jews searching for authentic Judaism"* (Yosef Rabinowitz, *The Book of Ezra*, x).

The rabbinic tradition praised Ezra highly; he is mentioned often in the Talmud. He was considered to be a man of Torah, as was Moses. It was observed that if Moses had not preceded him, Ezra would have received the Torah straight from Yahweh (B.T. *Sanhedrin* 21b-22a). Further, whereas God had given the Torah to the people through Moses, at a later time, when Torah was largely forgotten, Ezra acted to reestablish it in the Jewish community (B.T. *Sukkah* 20a-20b). In addition, a story circulated among the sages of the talmudic period that the survival of the Hebrew Scriptures was due to Ezra. After the sacred books were burned in the fall of Jerusalem, Ezra, so it was believed, was inspired by God to dictate to his assistants — for forty days — all the words found in the ruined books (4 Ezra 14:18-48).

The NT does not mention Ezra, but we should not immediately assume that he is fully absent simply because he is not mentioned. Recent NT scholarship is taking more seriously Jesus' roots in the Jewish traditions and his respect for Torah. In Matt. 23:2-3, Jesus declares: "The scribes and the Pharisees sit on Moses' seat; so practice and observe whatever they tell you." If these words represent the settled view of Jesus (or if these words are attributed to Jesus by a later writer who believes they represent Jesus' view of the Pharisees), then we may believe that some of the concerns of Ezra may have been those of Jesus as well.

NEHEMIAH IN LATER LITERATURE

Although Nehemiah is highly praised by Ben Sira in his listing of famous men (Sir. 49:13; Ezra is not mentioned!) and by the author of 2 Macc. 1:18, 20-36, the rabbis do not give him the fullsome praise they give to Ezra. In fact, some passages are sharply critical of him. For example, an early Jewish tradition considered the books of Ezra and Nehemiah to be one book, which was entitled "Ezra." This circumstance raised the question: Why was not a biblical book named for Nehemiah? The answer was twofold: He was too proud (see Neh. 13:31) and he was too critical of other leaders who served before him (see Neh. 5:15). Nevertheless, some in the rabbinic tradition appreciated him. For example, he was considered to be a prophet (B.T. *Berakoth* 13a), and he was associated with David and Hezekiah (B.T. *Sanhedrin* 93b-94a). Nehemiah's name is also absent from the NT, although Acts 4:24 probably alludes to Neh. 9:6. For further information on Ezra and Nehemiah in later literature, see Jacob M. Myers, *Ezra. Nehemiah*, LXXII-LXXVII; and *Encyclopedia Judaica* (under the names "Ezra" and "Nehemiah").

ABBREVIATIONS

ANET	*Ancient Near Eastern Texts Relating to the Old Testament*, ed. J. B. Pritchard, 3rd ed. 1969
B.C.E.	Before the Common Era (= B.C.)
B.T.	Babylonian Talmud
ca.	circa (about)
CBQ	*Catholic Biblical Quarterly*
C.E.	Common Era (= A.D.)
esp.	especially
Heb.	Hebrew
IDB	*Interpreter's Dictionary of the Bible*, ed. G.A. Buttrick, et al., 4 vols., 1962
JBL	*Journal of Biblical Literature*
JSOT	*Journal for the Study of the Old Testament*
JSS	*Journal of Semitic Studies*
lit.	literally
LXX	Septuagint
mg	Marginal note to the text of the RSV
MT	Masoretic Text (Hebrew)
NEB	New English Bible
OTS	*Oudtestamentische Studiën*
par.	parallel(s)
11QMelch	Melchizedek text from Qumran Cave 11
4QTestim	Testimonia text from Qumran Cave 4
RSV	Revised Standard Version
T. Judah	Testament of Judah
T. Levi	Testament of Levi
VT	*Vetus Testamentum*

The Book of
EZRA

INTERNATIONAL THEOLOGICAL COMMENTARY

George A.F. Knight and Fredrick Carlson Holmgren,
General Editors

ISRAEL ALIVE AGAIN
Ezra 1:1-11

GOD WORKS IN MYSTERIOUS WAYS (1:1)

Cyrus: Yahweh's Servant

The overthrow of Babylonian rule and the rise of the Persians under Cyrus in 539 B.C.E. sparked new hope in the eyes of the Jewish exiles. Even before the full collapse of the Babylonians, one prophet confidently predicted that Yahweh had chosen Cyrus to rescue and restore Israel. This prophet, whose oracles are recorded in Isa. 40–55, proclaimed deliverance and a new beginning to Israelites swept into slavery by the Babylonian army. God, he announced, would create this marvelous happening with the help of Cyrus, his "anointed" (i.e., his "messiah"; cf. Isa. 44:24-28, 45:1-6). During the era of this prophet (ca. 550-540 B.C.E.), who is commonly called Second Isaiah, Cyrus was beginning to emerge as the dominant military leader in the ancient Near East. Although an unlikely messiah to many, the prophet's hope was well placed. Eventually Cyrus, with the help of the Medes, defeated the Babylonians and, as a wise and humane king of the Persian empire, sent home again the many peoples that the Babylonians had deported. Not only did he resettle these many peoples in their homelands, but he also assisted them in reestablishing their temple worship. What Cyrus did for other captive nations, he did also for Israel. The decree of Cyrus, which the author of Ezra has paraphrased for Jewish readers in 1:2-4, is in full accord with Persian governmental policy.

The God Who Surprises Us

Sometimes help is found in unusual people and places. That Second Isaiah should see a Persian ruler serving Yahweh's purposes for Israel created questions in many minds (Isa. 45:9-13). But the prophet proved right. What a surprise! The Bible records many such surprises in life: Egyptian rulers were the salvation

3

of Joseph and his people; a Canaanite woman turns out to be more righteous than Judah the patriarch because of her daring act on behalf of her dead husband (Gen. 38:26); the princes of Judah, normally the opponents of Jeremiah, defend him when his life is threatened (Jer. 26:16); Gamaliel, a Pharisee, rescues the apostles from a mob (Acts 5:33-40); some Pharisees warn Jesus to flee for his life (Luke 13:31).

Cyrus belongs to this list of surprising people. Israelite priests and kings are the "anointed" or the "messiahs" of Yahweh (see Heb. *mashiah* in Lev. 4:l6; 1 Sam. 2:10) and so is Cyrus (Isa. 45:1). Similarly, just as Yahweh stirred up Israelites (i.e., awakened them to action; see Hag. 1:14; Ezra 1:5), so Yahweh "stirred up" Cyrus to make a decree that would allow the Jews to return to the land (Ezra 1:1). The God who acts is not restrained by the borders that separate Israelites from the rest of the world. God works for the good of his people through Cyrus, a foreign ruler. In fact, "Yahweh, the God of heaven," has given "all the kingdoms of the earth" to this Persian king (1:2). Although, in the text, these are words spoken by Cyrus, they are presented to us by the Jewish author who fully believes that Yahweh has chosen Cyrus and his successors as special servants to accomplish his will (cf. Ezra 6:22; 7:6, 27; Neh. 2:6).

"Yahweh Stirred up the Spirit of Cyrus"

The author does not explain *how* Yahweh "stirred up" (or "awakened") Cyrus to make a decree that allowed Jewish exiles to return home. This royal proclamation broke open a new future for the Jews. The Persian ruler's striking generosity (even if influenced by self-interest) was a mystery to our author. He could understand the decree of Cyrus only as evidence of God at work in the Persian empire. He does not, however, attempt to explain the mystery—and we should not assume that he has a simplistic view of God's relationship to the world. Although he attributes the release of the exiles to the work of God, surely he knows that charitable acts of this kind are not everyday occurrences. Tradition and experience must have made him fully aware of the presence of long-term, unrelieved suffering. In the midst of such oppression, people hope for release. One thinks of the hopes of those who were caught up in the Nazi horror or of people today who long for deliverance from cruel governments. *Sometimes deliverance comes—sometimes not.* The absence or presence of "divine" saving acts in the midst of evil resists understanding; it is not

4

fully predictable and cannot be convincingly explained by philosophical or theological argument.

Instead of an explanation, Ezra 1:1 offers a *witness* — it affirms that the decree of Cyrus is a shaft of light in the darkness of this world and which provides a glimpse of God's character and purpose for humankind. Abraham Heschel's comment is to the point: "The essence of Jewish religious thinking does not lie in entertaining a concept of God but in the ability to articulate a memory of moments of illumination by His presence. Israel is not a people of definers but a people of witnesses: 'Ye are My witnesses' (Isa. 43:10)" (*God in Search of Man: A Philosophy of Judaism*, 140).

The author of Ezra, together with Second Isaiah, bears witness to God's intervening act through Cyrus. By means of a foreign ruler, God expressed his loving-kindness to Israel! This "divine act" through Cyrus made a deep impress on the Jewish community; it helps us understand the positive view of the Persian rulers in the books of Ezra and Nehemiah. Frequently, the author of these books underscores the necessity of separation from foreigners whose presence would defile the community, but there is no rebuke, actual or implied, of Cyrus or any of the Persian rulers. The relationship is a positive one, and those returning to the land are expected to obey the law of God *and* the law of the Persian king (Ezra 7:26).

Crisis and Response

In times of crisis a community's response is not always a normative one. Sometimes, in order to survive, a community may involve itself in contradictory policies. Such is the case with the postexilic community. On the one hand, separation from all that is foreign is emphasized; on the other hand, there is appreciation for, and (limited) cooperation with, the Persian government. This twofold emphasis was an attempt to confront the community's chief problem: *survival*. It was recognized that the community would survive only if assimilation with peoples of other religious traditions was halted *and* if the community leadership cooperated with the Persian government. In normal times community leadership may have acted differently, but in a time when the life of the community was threatened, whatever promoted survival (short of repudiation of its basic beliefs) was done.

Jeremiah's Prophecy Fulfilled

The author of these lines considers the decree of Cyrus to be the beginning of the "accomplishment" of the prophetic word spoken by Jeremiah. The reference may be to a number of Jeremiah's oracles concerning the future, but uppermost in the author's mind (most likely) is Jeremiah's prophecy of a seventy-year captivity for the people of Judah (see Jer. 25:11; 29:10; cf. 2 Chron. 36:21). The number "seventy" should not be taken with any literalness; it is an approximate figure. Numbers in the Hebrew Bible are often inexact, traditional expressions. See, for example, the frequent occurrence of the following figures: three, seven, thirty, forty, and seventy.

The emphasis in v. 1, however, is not on the number "seventy," but on the *fact of restoration* which Jeremiah and others had confidently proclaimed. For many persons, the devastation of Jerusalem and the temple by the Babylonians, together with deportation, seemed to mark the end of the nation's life (cf. Lam. 5:22; Isa. 40:27; Ps. 89). Expectation of deliverance was not great. But then "there arose a new king over" the ancient world (see Exod. 1:8). In contrast to the one that arose in Egypt during Moses' time, this new king, Cyrus, replaced oppression (Isa. 47:6) with humaneness. It is an astonishing occurrence; there is release, a return to the land — a new beginning. Jeremiah is remembered as the one who forecasted this marvelous event. The narrator sees the prophet's oracle as a true word of God. Underneath the seeming matter-of-fact narrative of v. 1 lies a settled joy and confidence created by this wonder brought about by God — and Cyrus (cf. Ezra 6:14). The words are prose; the thought is poetry.

Jeremiah's Oracles: Not Completely Fulfilled

The restoration predicted by the prophets took place. Their oracles spoke the truth. We must be careful, however, not to overemphasize this point. The actual character of the restored community appears rather drab and incomplete when compared to the exalted language employed by the prophets to describe the coming age of restoration (cf., e.g., Jer. 30–31; Isa. 49:22-26; 54:1-17; Ezek. 37:15-28).

This gap between the prophecy and the fulfillment is explained, in part, by the hyperbolic language that the prophets used. Hyperbole often occurs in present-day speech ("I've told you a million times!") and was freely used by ancient writers. According to Paul, Christians sit with God "in the heavenly places in Christ Jesus" (Eph. 2:6). This image does not appear at first sight to fit the routine kind of life that often takes place within the Church. Yet it has meaning for Christians who know that something new and wonderful has come to them in Jesus Christ. Although the exaggerated language of the prophets appears to expect a more spectacular restoration movement than was actually the case, to many of those who participated in the return the prophets spoke the truth even if they were not "exactly right" concerning some aspects of Judah's future.

Reinterpretation of Jeremiah's Prophecy

However, it is clear to us — as it was to some later religious leaders in Israel — that the community formed by the returning exiles did not accomplish completely the words of Jeremiah or those of other prophets. Judah was not fully restored (Jer. 29:14; 30:18-21); she was not ruled over by her own king (Jer. 30:8-9, 21); the palace was not rebuilt in its former place (Jer. 30:18; contrast Ezekiel's view in 43:7-8); Judah did not become a power among the nations (Isa. 45:14; 49:22-23). This last hope was held to as late as the time of Haggai (520 B.C.E.), who envisioned Jewish supremacy under Zerubbabel (Hag. 2:4-9, 21-23).

This lack of *complete* fulfillment of the prophetic oracles moved some persons, including the author of Daniel, to regard the seventy-year prophecy of Jeremiah as standing unfulfilled. Daniel gives a new interpretation to Jeremiah's words. Zechariah (1:12), the Chronicler (2 Chron. 36:20-23), and apparently Ezra (1:1) thought the prophet meant approximately seventy years. But the author of Daniel understands Jeremiah to be speaking of "seventy weeks of years," that is, 490 years (Dan. 9:1-2, 24). Other, later writers also became convinced that Jeremiah's prophecy remained unfulfilled and made suggestions as to the "real" meaning of the oracle (see, e.g., 1 Enoch 85 – 90). Further, some people in our own day look to the future for the fulfillment of Jeremiah's seventh-century B.C.E. oracle.

The difference of opinion expressed by biblical authors concerning the understanding of Jeremiah's prophecy and its fulfillment underscores the diversity of opinion present in Scripture. A prophetic oracle, such as Jer. 29:10-14, may be interpreted (e.g., by Ezra 1:1) and then later be reinterpreted (e.g., by Dan. 9:2) without embarrassment. In the book of Ezekiel we have an example of a prophet reinterpreting one of his own oracles. Ezekiel prophesies that Nebuchadnezzar will completely destroy Tyre (ch. 26), but when the Babylonian king is unable to bring this about, the prophet changes his prophecy and offers Egypt to Nebuchadnezzar as compensation (Ezek. 29:17-20). Ezekiel makes no apology for this alteration. Biblical writers did not possess our firm philosophical doctrines of inspiration and authority.

Ezra 1:1 reflects the *elation* of a community of Jews who believed that God intervened at high levels to bring his people home again. The author does not subject Jeremiah's prophecy to searching analysis to see if the "fulfillment" matches completely the prophecy. He is not writing strict history; rather his words are the witness of a thankful heart. He remembers Jeremiah's words, and though the time period is not exact, they are words that affirm his own convictions: *the return was not by chance; Yahweh brought it about.* The witness of Ezra 1:1 is not nullified by the reinterpretation of a later writer.

THE DECREE OF CYRUS (1:2-6)

There are three representations of the decree of Cyrus in the Bible (Ezra 1:2-4; 2 Chron. 36:23; Ezra 6:3-5); the first two depict Cyrus as acknowledging that it is "Yahweh, the God of heaven" (Ezra 1:2), who has selected him to act on behalf of the Jews. But according to a Babylonian text, the Cyrus Cylinder, Cyrus views himself as the righteous ruler who is chosen by Marduk to restore the ancient worship of Babylon. Further, Cyrus speaks of his worship of Marduk and requests the gods to intercede on his behalf before the deities Bel and Nebo. It is probable that both the Hebrew and Babylonian texts are true reports of what happened, even though at first sight they appear to be contradictory. We know little of the personal faith of Cyrus; some scholars presume that he embraced the worship of Ahura Mazda as did his successors, but the issue is debated.

In any case, Cyrus was not a committed worshiper of Yahweh or Marduk. But neither did he regard Marduk and Yahweh as a threat to Persian religion or government. It may be that he conceived of them, together with other deities, as local representations of the God he himself worshiped. If this were the case, it is not surprising that when he addresses the Babylonians, he uses the name Marduk, and when he deals with Israel, he employs the name Yahweh.

"Yahweh, the God of Heaven"

The expression "the God of heaven" occurs twenty-two times in the Hebrew Bible — twelve of them in Ezra and Nehemiah. With the possible exception of Gen. 24:3, 7, this designation appears only in postexilic literature. It is a respected divine title within the Jewish community, as may be seen in the statement of Nehemiah (which was for Jewish ears only) that he fasted and prayed before "the God of heaven" (Neh. 1:4-5). But "God of heaven" reflects the affirmations of many religions in the ancient world and probably is to be seen as a somewhat neutral title. Jews and Persians are able to affirm each other by the use of this phrase while filling this title with meaning that is peculiar to their own beliefs. In its use, the Jews intend one meaning and the Persians another. For this reason we can well understand why the title is found mostly in contexts of Persian-Jewish communications.

The use of this ambiguous title in Ezra and Nehemiah is to be seen as a part of the general openness that the returning exiles maintained with the Persians. That the exiles were concerned to establish and preserve good relations with the Persians may be seen from: the lack of criticism of Persian rulers combined with a positive portrayal of them (Ezra 1:1-4; 7:12-26; Neh. 2:1-8); the apparent willingness of the Jews to include prayers for the king and his sons in temple worship (6:10); the absence of any definite statement attempting to exalt Yahweh above Persian deities or ridiculing these foreign gods (contrast the mockery of Babylonian gods in Isa. 41:18-20; 44:9-20; 46:1-2). We are looking in on a Jewish community which realizes that survival means getting along with the ruling power. The book of Esther also underscores this outlook in postexilic Judaism. During this period, the Jews struggled to maintain community integrity while cooperating with governmental leadership. Today, both Jewish and Christian communities know how difficult that struggle is. A thoughtless inflexibility that brings on governmental persecution is no more an answer than a thoughtless, assimilative policy that reflects little commitment to core religious traditions.

Ezra's use of the phrase "the God of heaven," especially in the context of Persian-Jewish communications, may exhibit a recognition of something authentic in Persian religion. It is apparent that the author of the book of Ezra believes that the Jews and Persians are talking about the same God (note that Artaxerxes designates Ezra "the priest, the scribe of the law of the God of heaven," Ezra 7:12), even though the two religions are quite different. This aspect of their relationship remains undeveloped in Ezra-Nehemiah. To say any more would be to say too much. But we may ask ourselves the question which is pressing for our own age: if non-Jewish and non-Christian religions do not in some manner reflect a genuine apprehension of the Jewish-Christian God, how are we to understand the appearance of justice, love, and grace within our world? (The discussion in the above several paragraphs owes much to the fine article of D. K. Andrews, "Yahweh the God of the Heavens," in *The Seed of Wisdom,* 45-57.)

The acceptance and appreciation of Persian rulers, as we have said, stands in contrast to the strict separatism enforced with regard to other people who dwelt in the land. But often we are less critical of "outsiders" who are far away from us than we are of those who are close — because those who are close represent a threat. See, for example, the case of the Gibeonites, who preserve themselves before the invading army of Joshua by declaring that they are "from a far country" (Josh. 9:6). If they had admitted that they were from the land, they would have been killed (see John Hamlin, *Joshua: Inheriting the Land,* 83-84).

Cyrus Allows Jews to Return to the Land

"Then rose up . . . every one whose spirit God had stirred [i.e., awakened to action]" (1:5). God stirs or inspires people to action in a variety of ways. Sometimes he calls to people through everyday objects and events. For example, Amos sees "a basket of summer fruit" (Amos 7:7) and Jeremiah sees an almond tree (Jer. 1:11-12); for both of them this "seeing" is a call to prophesy. The experiences of these two prophets are not foreign to us today. We also have heard God addressing us in the common experiences of life, for example, in a song, a courageous act, an unusual circumstance, happenings in the city, or the insightful words of a friend. The divine voice that Jeremiah and Amos "heard" in observing the almond tree and the summer fruit was heard by many of the Jewish exiles when the decree of Cyrus was made known. They recognized it as an act of God and saw in it God's call to resettle the land and to rebuild the temple.

Some Jews Did Not Return

The decree of Cyrus permitted Jews to return to the land, but not everyone desired to return. Many Jews remained, for example, in Babylonia. Some Jews heard the voice of God speaking through the decree, saying: "Return." Others apparently heard no such voice for themselves. They remained in Babylon or in other lands where they had now lived for more than half a century. No doubt, some may have separated themselves from Jewish traditions during the Exile and therefore had little interest in or sympathy for those who returned to the land. But others remained behind in Babylon ("men of his place," v. 4; "all who were about them," v. 6) and assisted the returning adventurers in rebuilding the temple by their gifts of silver, gold, and freewill offerings.

Those Who Remained in Babylon

In our admiration for the Jews who returned to rebuild the temple and Jerusalem, we should not forget the contribution to the life of faith made by those who remained in Babylon. Although our knowledge of the Babylonian Jewish community is sparse, its contribution to later Judaism testifies of a strong commitment to Israel's traditions. When Jews today speak of the Talmud, they almost always are referring to the Babylonian Talmud, that extensive body of teaching that was compiled and developed by Babylonian scholars from ca. 100 B.C.E. to 600 C.E. There is a Palestinian Talmud, but it has never had the commanding respect given to the former. Jews who remained in Babylon enriched greatly the life of later Judaism.

Today many of us admire the heroic Jews who have given their lives to establish a Jewish state, Israel. Their efforts have had a profound effect on Jews as well as non-Jews. But diaspora Judaism (Jews who live outside Israel) now, as in the postexilic period, continues to support the homeland and carries on those teachings rooted in the Hebrew Bible. Without diaspora Judaism the present-day Jewish witness would lose much of its richness. The continuing importance of diaspora Judaism to the life of faith makes us cautious in our judgment of those who stayed behind when the first exiles returned to the land in the later 6th century B.C.E. While we are impressed by the courage and devotion of those who returned, we cannot view as disobedient those who stayed behind to live out their life of faith in Babylon. Notice that there is no criticism in Ezra-Nehemiah of those who did not make ʿaliyah (i.e., immigrate to Israel). Those who do not hear God calling them to do what others are doing are not necessarily wrong.

Did Gentiles Help Jews to Return?

Some scholars differ from the above interpretation of the phrases "men of his place" and "all who were about them." They assume that these phrases refer to non-Jewish neighbors. According to this view, the writer of vv. 2-6 wished to represent the return to Jerusalem from Babylon as a second Exodus, as did the Prophet of the Exile (Isa. 40–55). An example of this intent, they say, is revealed when the author represents non-Jews in Babylon (i.e., "men of his place" and "all who were about them") as giving gifts to the returning Jews. This act on the part of the non-Jews would parallel what happened during the first Exodus, when the Egyptians gave presents of silver, gold, and clothing to speed the departure of the people of Israel (Exod. 12:35-36). This interpretation is possible, but unlikely, even though there appears to be a "second Exodus" theme elsewhere in the book of Ezra (see our comments in ch. 8).

Building the Tabernacle and the Temple

The major motif in Ezra 1:2-6 is the rebuilding of the temple. If there is any reference here to the Exodus period, it is to the building of the tabernacle, *not* to the Exodus event itself when the Egyptians gave "going away" gifts to the Hebrews. Ezra 1:5-6 indicates that the leaders of the people (including the priests and Levites, who had special concern for the temple) returned "to rebuild the house of the LORD which is in Jerusalem," and they were supported in their efforts by "all who were about them" (i.e., Jews), who gave gifts of silver, gold, and freewill offerings. Those who finally returned to the land also offered the same gifts (Ezra 2:68-69). It was this kind of cooperative effort among the early Israelites that enabled the tabernacle to be built, according to Exod. 35–36. Skilled people were appointed by God to construct the tabernacle (Exod. 35:30–36:5), and these artisans were aided in their work by the gifts of the people, which included gold, silver, valuables of all kinds, and freewill offerings (Exod. 35:5, 22-24, 29; 36:3; cf. Ezra 1:4, 6).

Our comments relating the rebuilding of the temple to the construction of the tabernacle in the period of the Exodus suggest the following observation. The exciting and important parts of the book of Exodus to the modern reader are those sections that speak of the deliverance from Egypt and the giving of the Torah at Sinai. Those passages that describe the building of the tabernacle and the formation of the cult are reckoned to be of much lesser value—and boring. The books of Ezra and Nehemiah appear unimportant for similar reasons; they deal with the reformation and rebuilding of the cultic community. But it must not be overlooked that *revelatory events only continue to be revelatory through the formation of some kind of community structure which "remembers" the event* and reflects on its implications for life. Although "institutionalization" is always a danger for revelation and faith, it contributes to their survival.

THE TEMPLE VESSELS ARE RETURNED (1:7-11)

When Nebuchadnezzar conquered Judah, he did what many other conquerors had done: he removed a large portion of the population to his own homeland in order to prevent an uprising, and he brought back to Babylon the sacred temple objects. These "vessels" *(kelim),* which were once used in the service of Yahweh, the God of Israel, were at one time under the control of the gods worshiped by Nebuchadnezzar, king of Babylon. Nebuchadnezzar's transfer of these "vessels" to Babylon symbolized the superiority of the Babylonian gods over Yahweh. It was this superiority that Babylon could flaunt on occasion, possibly in a way similar to the incident recorded in Dan. 5:1-4. This passage records the arrogant act of Belshazzar, who celebrated the power of the gods of Babylon while drinking from the sacred temple vessels. But Babylon's rule was brief; after some seventy years she collapsed and was succeeded by the Persians, whose first king was Cyrus.

The Persians: Enlightened Self-Interest

The city and temple that Nebuchadnezzar's army had destroyed was rebuilt through the generous support of the Persian government. The people and cultic objects, taken away by the Babylonians, were returned to the land by Cyrus under the leadership of Sheshbazzar (cf. 1:8, 11; see the discussion of Sheshbazzar in ch. 3). The Persians treated other captured peoples similarly. It appears that Cyrus and his successors took this "considerate" action out of enlightened self-interest. It represented an attempt to pacify certain potentially troubled areas (see the excellent article of Amelie Kuhrt, "The Cyrus Cylinder and Achaemenid Imperial Policy," *JSOT* 25 [1983]: 83-97, esp. 92-93). But even if the decree of Cyrus was proclaimed out of enlightened self-interest (a consideration that often has produced significant good in the world), it had a touch of humaneness and generosity. To the returned exiles it spoke of the action of God. It is not surprising, therefore, that Jewish writings have little if any criticism of Cyrus and the Persian government. This positive attitude toward the Persian overlord stands in contrast with the image of Babylon in Jewish and Christian literature. Babylon, together with Egypt, becomes a symbol of evil (cf. Isa. 47; Jer. 51; 1 Pet. 5:13; Rev. 14:8; 17:5).

THE EXILES RETURN TO THE LAND
Ezra 2:1-70

A SELECTIVE HISTORY

Several prophets had spoken enthusiastically about the return of the exiles to their homeland (e.g., Jer. 50:17-20; Ezek. 20:33-44). The most enthusiastic and colorful oracles on this theme come from Second Isaiah. Frequently he described the return to the land as a new Exodus (e.g., Isa. 48:20-21; 52:11-12). We do not possess, however, many hard facts about the character of the exilic community or the character of the return journey to the land. Why did some go and others stay? Did all the exiles return together in one group, or did they return to the land in small groups over a period of time? Was the new Exodus as marvelous as that described in Isa. 40–55?

The author of Ezra and Nehemiah has little interest in these matters. His focus of attention is on the character of the community formed by the returning exiles. But even here he is selective. He tells us almost nothing about the great leaders of that period, Sheshbazzar, Zerubbabel, and Jeshua (see our discussion of them in ch. 3). It is apparent that he is not writing to satisfy our thirst for information about this period. His great concern is to demonstrate that God is with those who establish and preserve a pure society. A "pure society" means, positively, loyalty to Yahweh through obedience to Torah and proper temple worship. Negatively, a "pure society" means separation from people who would pollute the community.

These Are the People Who Belong

Western, non-Jewish readers frequently have little appreciation for the genealogical lists in the Bible (see, e.g., 1 Chron. 1–9; Ezra 8). They are boring to us not only because the names are ancient and unfamiliar, but also because they represent a different

14

way of looking at life. Modern, Western civilization places great emphasis on the individual; ancient societies (and some modern ones), however, give first importance to the family and clan. In the latter kind of society there are no free-floating individuals. Everyone is a member of some family and comes from some place. The individual understands himself in terms of that family, and he is known and valued by others as an individual who comes from this particular place. The character of every individual is known by his background, because (it was believed) his ancestors live on through him. Naturally, the presence of a non-Israelite family (and, in the case of postexilic Judaism, a non-Jewish family) in the genealogy would raise serious questions because an individual in this line could carry these foreign elements into the community. As may be seen in Ezra 2:59-63, the issue of descent was an extremely important issue for the Jews who were establishing themselves in the land.

Genealogy and Membership in Israel

Genealogical information was important to ancient Israel because it protected the community from the disruptive person — the person who would bring ruin to the community. This screening by genealogy did not always work because some individuals did not live up to the character of their ancestors. But for the most part it was believed that those who came from established Jewish families would be good members of the community. Although exceptions were recognized, Israel shared the belief with other ancient societies that "the apple does not fall far from the tree" (cf. Prov. 22:6).

Synagogue and Church Membership

In our day many churches and synagogues share the concern of the postexilic Jewish community. These congregations do not want to allow into membership those people who are not committed to their central beliefs. One purpose of membership requirements in synagogues and churches is to screen persons desiring to become members of the congregation. The requirements may be flexible and generous, but all the same the requirements are there to preserve the core beliefs of the community from those who may change them.

A community that gives no attention to the preservation of its traditions may lose its character — its life. But a community that focuses too much on its particularity may also suffer loss by becoming so exclusivistic that it refuses to receive people who deserve to be welcomed. Not surprisingly, a community under threat and living on the edge of existence is tempted to embrace the latter policy.

Genealogy: A Reminder of God's Grace

In addition to the negative aspect of genealogical lists, about which we have spoken at some length, there is a positive side. People who are descendants of the families named in these lists are reminded that they belong to a select community — the people of Israel whom Yahweh has chosen as his own people. Charles Kraft's remarks on a conversation between a Gentile and a Jewish student are to the point (*Christianity in Culture*, 229): "The Gentile asked the Jewish student what his favorite passage of Scripture was. His immediate response was, 'The first eight chapters of First Chronicles.' These are Hebrew genealogies. From my (Gentile) point of view I have often wondered why God allowed so much space in his Word to be 'wasted' on such trivia. But to a Hebrew (and to many other kinship-oriented societies around the world) *genealogical lists of this nature demonstrate in the clearest way the specificity of God's love and concern that lies at the heart of the Gospel*" (emphasis mine).

The genealogical listings in 1 Chronicles, Ezra, and Nehemiah underscore dramatically the words spoken to Moses by Yahweh: "Now therefore, if you will obey my voice and keep my covenant, you shall be my own possession among all peoples; for all the earth is mine, and you shall be to me a kingdom of priests and a holy nation" (Exod. 19:5-6).

Including and Excluding

Ezra-Nehemiah is describing a community that has formed itself around Jewish families that were in exile. The leaders make a serious attempt to keep out those who do not qualify, but they also try to include all who do belong. This concern of the community is seen in the cases of individuals who declare that they are Jewish exiles but who are unable to prove it. They are not immediately cast out. Final decision on them was to be made by a priest who would consult the Urim and Thummim (2:59-63).

The community appears to be very strict on the matter of membership — *and it was,* but we must take care that we do not exaggerate the strictness. *Most individuals and communities make room for exceptions.* For example, the narratives concerning Elijah and Elisha depict these two prophets as zealots for Yahweh. They call the people to choose for Yahweh or against him (see, e.g., 1 Kgs.

16

18:21); they demand a radical decision. Certainly, we believe, they will not do or say anything that even approaches compromise. These stories do not prepare us for the final exchange between Elisha and Naaman in 2 Kgs. 5:17-19. Naaman has made a clear decision to serve Yahweh; he pledges to sacrifice only to the God of Elisha. With regard to sacrifice, however, he has a problem: " 'In this matter may the LORD pardon your servant: when my master goes into the house of Rimmon to worship there, leaning on my arm, and I bow myself in the house of Rimmon, when I bow myself in the house of Rimmon, the LORD pardon your servant in this matter.' He said to him, 'Go in peace.' " If this passage were not in the Bible we could never imagine that Elisha would respond in this understanding manner. His word to Naaman is unexpected; it does not appear to be in harmony with his demand for an uncompromised decision for Yahweh.

Perhaps if we knew more about the community of the returned exiles, we would find out that it was not quite as rigid as we have imagined. Ezra 6:21 points in this direction. It refers to some people, not belonging to the Jewish exiles (proselytes? people of Judah who remained in the land?), as participants in the community Passover.

The True Israel: The Exiles

Although we must allow for the possibility of exceptions and modifications, the community of Israel that forms in the land following the decree of Cyrus is limited (for the most part) to Jews who had been in exile. But Ezra and Nehemiah were not the first to identify the Jewish exiles as the true Israel. Earlier prophets had made the same judgment. For example, Jeremiah considered the Jews who went into exile to be the "good figs" as opposed to those who remained in the land, whom he labeled "bad figs" (Jer. 24:1-10). Ezekiel also addresses this issue. He believes that the people who were left behind in the land were so wicked that Yahweh was forced to leave his temple (Ezek. 8:6) and journey to Babylon to be with his people (11:22-25). Neither Jeremiah nor Ezekiel was fully pleased with the exiles (cf. Jer. 29:15-32 and Ezek. 12:1-3), but apparently they were preferable to those living in the land.

Although the earlier prophets viewed the Jewish exiles as those who most truly made up the people of Israel, it was left to other, later leaders to indicate what this would mean for the community that formed after the Exile. Some practical questions needed to be answered. Who belongs to this community? Who is permitted to work on the temple? Who may take part in the temple worship? The answer of the community's leadership was: the Jewish exiles who had returned. Given their preference for the exiles, Jeremiah and Ezekiel may have had more sympathy for the program of Ezra and Nehemiah than we imagine.

The Names: Religious Significance

This long list of names appears to have a religious *and* a political significance. As we have already indicated, it serves a religious purpose in that it establishes the identity of those who belong to the congregation of Israel. The list, which is headed by twelve names (cf. the parallel passage in Neh. 7:7; Ezra 2:2 has only 11 names), indicates that the community thinks of itself as continuing in some manner the tradition of the twelve-tribe league of early Israel.

The Names: Political Significance

In addition to the religious significance, the list has a legal or political purpose. The decree of Cyrus assigned responsibility for the rebuilding of the temple to the exiles (Ezra 1:2-4). Offers of help from people who did not belong to the exilic group were refused (4:1-3). The refusal was probably for religious reasons, that is, fear of foreign religious traditions, but the Jews based it on legal grounds, that is, on the decree of Cyrus which specified that only the exiles were to build the temple (1:3). Although the refusal created anger and opposition, the legal base for the refusal was solid.

At one point, Tattenai, governor of the Persian province, inspected the building project and asked: "Who gave you a decree to build this house and to finish this structure?" and "What are the names of the men who are building this building?" (Ezra 5:3-4). The decree of Cyrus provided an answer to the first question, and the list of names in Ezra 2 / Neh. 7 covered the second. For further discussion, see the following articles, which are reflected in the above paragraphs: Kurt Galling, "The 'Gola List' according to Ezra 2 // Nehemiah 7," *JBL* 70 (1951): 149-58; and Carl Schultz, "The Political Tensions Reflected in Ezra-Nehemiah," in *Scripture in Context*, 221-44 (esp. 225-30).

Second Isaiah and Ezra

This description of the restored community appears dull beside the dramatic poetry of Second Isaiah. His colorful and exuberant language excites our faith. Yahweh is on the move with his people — leading them in a new Exodus (Isa. 52:8-12). He is a God of great power (40:18-26) but also most tender to those worn down by captivity (40:27-31). Opposed to the institutionalism which confronts us in Ezra 2 stands the open and intimate relationship between Yahweh and people in Second Isaiah (e.g., 43:1-7; 54:5-8). It is a temptation to think that if this prophet had lived to guide the restored community, his program would have been quite different from that of Ezra and Nehemiah. Maybe, but then again, maybe not.

Second Isaiah directed his oracles to a discouraged, captive people. He spoke to them of release and return to the land, but he knew that all of this was preparation for the full redemption, that is, the reinstitution of the temple community in Jerusalem. Those who take part in the new Exodus from Babylon will carry with them the sacred "vessels of the LORD" (Isa. 52:11). Presumably, he believed that they would be placed in the new temple that would be rebuilt (44:28) and would be used by the personnel of the temple. In short, Second Isaiah must have envisioned a good part of the program that actually was instituted when the exiles returned (including priests, Levites, and temple servants).

The difference between the Exilic Prophet and the leadership of the restored community has to do, to some extent, with a matter of emphasis. On the one hand, Second Isaiah speaks of the glory of the release from captivity and the downfall of Babylon, but says nothing specific about what is to be done when the exiles reach the land. On the other hand, the books of Ezra and Nehemiah focus on the restored community in the land; they do not give any space to the drama of the return itself. Although we cannot say that Second Isaiah would have agreed fully with the policies of the later leaders of the restored community, it appears that he would have supported the establishment of a temple community. It is also likely that the preexilic prophets, such as Isaiah and Jeremiah, would also have endorsed the erection of a new temple. For all their critical words against the temple and its personnel, we should not imagine that they thought the cultic aspect of Israel's life was unimportant. See the next chapter for a continuation of the discussion on the cultic aspect of the restored community.

By returning to the land to establish a new temple community, the Jews announced their refusal to let the Babylonian devastation bring an end to the traditions that had nourished the families of Parosh, Shephatiah, Arah, and others (Ezra 2:3-5). They believed that the past deserved a future and they determined to work with God to create that future.

19

BEGINNING AGAIN
Ezra 3:1-13

OUTER AND INNER RELIGION:
SOME GENERAL COMMENTS

Read by itself, this chapter may support the popular view that leaders of the postexilic period emphasized external religion. It takes on a different cast, however, when viewed against the background of preexilic faith. Previous to the Exile, life in south Israel (Judah) centered in the temple at Jerusalem. Here, in this place of sacrifice, prayer, and singing, served the priests and other cultic personnel. Although we lack detailed knowledge about the various rituals of temple worship, we learn something of the character of this worship through the Psalms, which have their setting in the temple cultus. The piety reflected in this ancient poetry, nourished in the context of animal sacrifices, offerings, and festal gatherings, has an enduring appeal to both Jews and Christians. The God of the Psalms is the gracious One who accepts us as we are, who loves us and remains with us when those closest to us leave. The God of the Psalms is Immanuel—God with us.

The Temple: God's Dwelling Place

This loving, saving God, who rejoices the heart of the psalmist, is "present" in the temple. His "glory" and "name" are there (1 Kgs. 8:11, 29). The worshiper yearns for the temple because in this sacred place he has experienced the divine presence.

> How lovely is thy dwelling place,
>> O LORD of hosts!
> My soul longs, yea, faints
>> for the courts of the LORD. (Ps. 84:1-2)
>
> O LORD, I love the habitation of thy house,
>> and the the place where thy glory dwells. (Ps. 26:8)

Many Jews in exile remembered the temple and Jerusalem with pain and deep love (Ps. 137:1-6). So intimate was the relationship between God and the temple that they could not imagine a restoration that did not include a new temple. Ezekiel and Second Isaiah were of a similar mind. Ezekiel envisions a future when the temple community (with some changes) will exist once more (Ezek. 40–48). As we noticed in the last chapter, Second Isaiah speaks of the redemption of the exiles in terms of a new Exodus. He does not believe, however, that this deliverance will be complete until Jerusalem is rebuilt, the temple restored (Isa. 44:26-28), and the "vessels of the LORD" returned to Zion (Isa. 52:11). Further, often his language reflects the priestly speech of the temple (see, e.g., the priestly oracle of salvation in Isa. 41:14; 43:1). It is not too much to believe that he, like many others, longed "for the courts of the LORD" (Ps. 84:2).

In summary, when we read ch. 3 of Ezra, we should think of the piety of the book of Psalms that includes expressions of love for the temple itself. We should think also of the exiles who were driven from their homeland and separated from worship and the religious traditions that gave meaning to their lives. They remembered the temple as the "house" of Yahweh. To be sure, they experienced God in other places and events, *but in this particular place* were the memories, traditions, symbols, people, and rituals which nourished their lives.

FIRST THINGS FIRST:
THE ALTAR AND SACRIFICES (3:1-7)

Immediately, in the first year of the return (538 B.C.E), the altar is set up so that the burnt offerings may be made. Although the sacrifice of animals may be repugnant to people today, it was not to the prophets, nor was it offensive to Jesus. Although both Jesus and the prophets are critical of those who substitute sacrifices for basic morality, neither of them speaks against sacrifice itself. Such acts were accepted acts of worship at that time. We must look beyond the physical, violent act of killing an animal to the meaning underlying it.

The Burnt Offering

The burnt (or whole) offering (Heb. *olah* — that which goes up) is the chief sacrifice of the OT. The animal is completely burnt. Neither priest nor worshiper eats of it; in its entirety it "goes up" to God. The ritual enacted for this kind of sacrifice provides that the one who offers it should place his hand on the head of the animal (Lev. 1:4). In so doing, the worshiper identifies himself

21

with the animal, that is, he is offering himself to God. Thus the sacrificial act is a symbolic action. In burning the *whole* animal — which goes up *wholly* to God — the worshiper is declaring his *wholehearted* devotion to God. In presenting burnt offerings to Yahweh, even before the foundation of the temple was laid (v. 6), the returnees displayed their earnestness to be "a living sacrifice to God" (Rom. 12:1).

In addition to being a wholehearted commitment to Yahweh, the burnt offering was a plea for God's saving presence — a presence that the Jews fervently sought "for fear was upon them because of the peoples of the lands" (v. 3). We are not told why the Jews feared these "peoples of the lands," who apparently were foreigners (cf. Ezra 9:1-2), but they seem to have posed a threat to them. The intimidating presence of these people may have been an important motive for the quick construction of the altar. This is the first hint of opposition to the Jews; the opposition becomes stronger and more determined as work continues on the temple and then, later, on the walls about Jerusalem.

LAYING THE FOUNDATIONS (3:8-13)

In the above verses Zerubbabel and Jeshua (spelled "Joshua" in Haggai and Zechariah) are given the credit for the laying of the temple foundations. In Ezra 5:16, however, it is said that Sheshbazzar (cf. also 1:8, 11) "laid the foundations of the house of God which is in Jerusalem." The accomplishments of these three leaders and their relationship to each other are difficult to define. As we noted above, the author has written a selective history of the restored community, and, for reasons best known to him, he chose not to give the reader much information concerning these three men. We know that they were influential leaders in the early years of the return, but we can only make conjectures about their relationships to each other and some of their accomplishments.

Sheshbazzar

Sheshbazzar, who possesses a Babylonian name, is identified as "the prince *[nasi]* of Judah" (Ezra 1:8) and as a "governor" appointed by Cyrus (Ezra 5:14). Outside of the book of Ezra he is never mentioned. According to information preserved in this book, Sheshbazzar led the first group of exiles back to the land and was in charge of the temple vessels (1:8, 11; 5:14-15). Further, he is designated as the one who "laid the foundations of the house of God" (5:16). That he was appointed governor, a title held also by

Zerubbabel (Hag. 1:1) and Tattenai (Ezra 5:3), indicates that the Persians looked upon him as a significant person.

His other title, "the prince of Judah," marks him as a Jewish leader. What this title *(nasi)* implies is not certain. It is used of Abraham (Gen. 23:6), tribal chieftains (Num. 1:16, 44; RSV "leaders"), King Zedekiah (Ezek. 12:10, 12), and the future Davidic ruler (Ezek. 34:24; 37:25; 44:3). Although the title is used of non-royal persons, it is possible that "prince of Judah" indicates that Sheshbazzar is of royal blood and is descended from David. The Ezekiel passages referred to above and Sheshbazzar's leadership in laying the foundations of the temple (a royal function which calls Solomon to mind) point in this direction. Attempts to prove his Davidic lineage by identifying him with Shenazzar, son of King Jeconiah (1 Chron. 3:17-18), or with Zerubbabel, are not convincing. We have no further knowledge of Sheshbazzar's past nor are we given any information about what happened to him after the foundations of the temple were laid.

Zerubbabel

We can be more certain about the identity of Zerubbabel, who also possesses a Babylonian name ("Seed of Babylon"). But in his case too our information is limited. He is the son of Shealtiel (3:2, 8), who is the son of Jeconiah, that is, Jehoiachin, king of Judah (1 Chron. 3:17). Thus Zerubbabel is of Davidic descent. He is mentioned (often with Jeshua/Joshua) in Ezra (2:2; 3:2, 8; 4:2, 3; 5:2), Nehemiah (7:7; 12:1), 1 Chron. 3:19, Haggai (1:1, 12, 14; 2:3, 5, 24), and Zechariah (4:6, 7, 9, 10; cf. 3:8 and 6:9-14).

Zerubbabel's relationship to Sheshbazzar is unclear. Both have the title "governor" (Ezra 1:8 — Sheshbazzar; Hag. 1:1 — Zerubbabel). Sheshbazzar led a group of exiles back to the land (Ezra 1:8, 11), as did Zerubbabel (Ezra 2:2; cf. 3:8). Further, both are remembered as having had a part in working on the foundations of the temple in the time of Cyrus, ca. 537 B.C.E. (Ezra 3:8-13; 5:16). A complicating bit of information occurs in Hag. 1:13-15 and 2:18. These passages date Zerubbabel's work on the foundations of the temple in the time of Darius rather than in the period of Cyrus (i.e., after 520 B.C.E.). It is not impossible, of course, that both Sheshbazzar and Zerubbabel worked on the foundations of the temple in the time of Cyrus but were forced to quit because of strong opposition (see Paul Hanson, *Dawn of Apocalyptic*, 243-44, who makes this suggestion concerning Sheshbazzar; cf. Zech. 8:9-10). One could then assume that later on, in the time of Darius, Zerubbabel completed the work on the foundations of the temple. The difficulty with that view, however, is that the report in Haggai reveals no awareness of any earlier work on the temple by Zerubbabel or Sheshbazzar, even though Ezra 3:10 speaks of an earlier celebration at the time when the foundations were laid.

Another possible explanation of the conflicting passages is to assume that the writer of Ezra, who wrote over a hundred years after the events described, may have made a chronological error, that is, he believed that the laying of the foundation was completed by Zerubbabel in 537 B.C.E. (in the time of Cyrus), when in fact it did not take place until some twenty years later, in the time of Darius (ca. 516 B.C.E.; cf. Hag. 1:14). These slips are easy to make and, although they do not happen frequently in the Bible, they do occur now and then (see, e.g., Mark 2:26, where the Gospel writer identifies Abiathar as the priest who befriended David, when actually it was Ahimelech; cf. 1 Sam. 21:1-6).

Zerubbabel and Jeshua

From the books of Haggai and Zechariah (where "Jeshua" is spelled "Joshua"), we know that great expectations were associated with Zerubbabel and Jeshua. Haggai declares that Yahweh is about to "overthrow the throne of kingdoms" (Hag. 2:22). In that day, he announces, Yahweh will make Zerubbabel "like a signet ring" (i.e., he will have Yahweh's authority behind him), because Yahweh has "chosen" him and made him his "servant" (Hag. 2:23). Yahweh assures Zerubbabel and Joshua that in this new time (when he will "shake the heavens and the earth"; Hag. 2:6, 21), "the treasures of all nations shall come, and I will fill this house [i.e., the temple] with splendor" (Hag. 2:7).

Did Haggai and Zechariah look upon Zerubbabel as the one to reestablish the monarchy? He was of the family of David, as mentioned above, but nothing is said of his Davidic descent in Haggai or Zechariah. Further, he is not even given the title of "prince" *(nasi),* as was Sheshbazzzar. Nevertheless, it is clear that royal and messianic expectations were associated with him. However, the references to Zerubbabel in Ezra and Nehemiah contain no allusions to this kind of role. We are given no information about what happened to him. He is like a bright star that shines brilliantly for a while and then disappears.

Controversy over Zerubbabel

As we read about Zerubbabel in the above biblical books, we may be looking upon a controversy taking place in postexilic

Judaism. In the exilic and postexilic periods, an old issue confronted the community: *Should the people of Yahweh have a human king to rule over them?* It was an issue fiercely debated in early Israel. At that time, some believed that the selection of a king was an act of apostasy (Judg. 8:22-23; 1 Sam. 8:4-9).

With the rise of David's rule the tradition develops that Yahweh himself has made a covenant with David in which he promises to establish a Davidic dynasty over Israel that will never cease (1 Sam. 7). When Judah's king (Jehoiachin) was taken captive at the fall of Jerusalem in 597 B.C.E., it appeared that God had failed to keep his promise. Nevertheless, some Judeans appealed to God for renewal of the kingship, hoping that this tragic event was but a brief interruption (see Ps. 89). But others gave up completely on a restored monarch. For example, Second Isaiah speaks of a covenant that Yahweh is making with the *people* of Judah in his day (Isa. 55:3-5). He considers it to be a continuation of the covenant that Yahweh made with David, but this time there will be no "David" to mediate the covenant to the people; Yahweh will make this covenant directly with the people.

Ezekiel's View of Kingship

Ezekiel represents an intermediate position with regard to the monarchy. He does not believe that the monarchy has come to an end, but the one that he expects to rule over the postexilic community will not have the power of the preexilic monarchs. Ezekiel depicts a ruler (a "prince"; *nasi*) whose power is second to the Zadokite priests. He clearly lacks the prerogatives of the preexilic king (Ezek. 46:1-18).

Zerubbabel in Haggai and Zechariah

Haggai and Zechariah continue the stance of Ezekiel; they speak of two leaders in the postexilic community, namely, Zerubbabel and Joshua (Hag. 1:1, 14; Zech. 4:6-10). Although great things are spoken of Zerubbabel, one should not miss the fact that *he shares rule with Joshua the high priest — a Zadokite* (see Ezekiel's emphasis on Zadokite rule in Ezek. 40:15-31). When Zerubbabel finally disappears, Joshua the high priest becomes the ruler — an indication of the power of his person. We do not know the reason for Zerubbabel's sudden departure. The usual suggestion, that the Persians removed him because they feared that he would lead a revolt, is possible. But considering the growing power of the priests in the exilic and postexilic communities, it may be that Joshua the high priest had such power that he was able to exclude

25

Zerubbabel and rule alone (so, e.g., H. Jagersma, *A History of Israel in the Old Testament Period,* 198).

Jeremiah's Oracle and Zerubbabel

Zerubbabel's rise and disappearance raise a question about the "authority" of an oracle announced by Jeremiah. He declared that no descendants of Coniah (i.e., King Jehoiachin) will ever reign over Israel (Jer. 22:30). But Zerubbabel is a relative of Jehoiachin; he is the son of Shealtiel, who is the son of Jehoiachin (Ezra 3:2 and 1 Chron. 3:17). The prophet's words stand opposed to the dreams that Haggai and Zechariah had for Zerubbabel. Jeremiah's oracles concerning the future may have been highly regarded in the postexilic period (see, e.g., the seventy-year prophecy which is alluded to in Ezra 1:1; 1 Chron. 36:22; Zech. 1:12; and Dan. 9:2). It is possible, therefore, that the prophet's words against Jehoiachin and his descendants created such opposition to Zerubbabel that he was driven from power. It may be, however, that Jeremiah's words were not understood in such a literalistic sense. In any case, by the time of Jesus the words of Jeremiah were no longer influential, for according to the NT writers (Luke 1:31-32; cf. Jer. 22:30), he who will sit on the throne of David is descended from David through Jehoiachin (Matt. 1:11-12).

A Revised View of Zerubbabel: Ezra and Nehemiah

Zerubbabel is mentioned in Ezra and Nehemiah but only as a leader of those who returned and as one responsible for laying the foundations of the temple. These writings do not hint of the expectations that surrounded him at an earlier time, that is, as a new Davidic ruler. The departure of Zerubbabel without fulfilling the hopes of Haggai and Zechariah must have caused great pain to those who had set their hopes on him. The pain was there—surely—but it is not expressed anywhere in Scripture. This bitterly disappointing experience with Zerubbabel was erased from Jewish memory, and the people looked for other manifestations of divine activity.

In Haggai and Zechariah, Zerubbabel appears as a threat to the nations, which would include Persia also. Yahweh will destroy "the strength of the kingdoms of the nations" (Hag. 2:22), after which Zerubbabel will be exalted as the special servant of Yahweh (Hag. 2:23). For the author of Ezra and Nehemiah, that is all in the past now. The community represented in these books is thoroughly cooperative with the Persians; there is no threat of revolution against the Persians nor of the destruction of surrounding nations. Some Jews must have felt that this cooperation was in fact apostate collaboration. However, such a view finds no expression in the OT.

Scripture does not give any detailed, absolute rules on the relationship of the faith community to the secular power, except the general one that has a place in both the Jewish and Christian traditions, that is, obedience to God supercedes any demand of the state (Acts 5:29; B.T. *Sanhedrin* 49a). But in certain situations this principle is not fully helpful, because people have always had different opinions as to what it means to be obedient to God!

The Lord Is Good

The song that Israel sings has many verses — verses that express pain, despair, anger, joy, sorrow, hope, and fear — but the chorus of the song is usually the same: "For he is good, for his steadfast love endures for ever toward Israel" (v. 11). To the accompaniment of trumpets and cymbals the priests and Levites sing the chorus responsively. It is a joyous occasion "because the foundation of the house of the LORD was laid" (v. 11). But there were older people attending the celebration who remembered what the earlier temple was like. The repaired foundation did not at all compare to the original one. Although they probably rejoiced with others to see a new temple building on its way, they could not restrain themselves from weeping when they thought of the first temple (v. 12). By modern standards that temple was not very large (at most, 165 ft. by 82 ft.) but it had been a treasured shrine for the elders. The new temple was to be of approximately the same size (Ezra 2:68; see the phrase "erect it on its site").

Although large stones were used in the repair of the foundation (Ezra 5:8; 6:4), they may not have compared to the massive ones used in Solomon's temple. In any case, a repaired foundation and temple would not likely have the grandeur of the original; marks of its ruin would probably remain. No doubt any new temple erected would have failed to heal the hurt in the hearts of those who knew the first temple. Even if the artisans had been able to reset the foundation stones so that they would have compared well with the first temple, what artisan can restore the memories of a former day?

EFFECTIVE OPPOSITION
Ezra 4:1-24

MEMBERS OF THE OPPOSITION (4:1-5)

This whole chapter concentrates on the strong opposition that the Jews faced when they began to rebuild the temple. We are not, however, fully informed about the nature of the opposition or the people involved.

Ezra 4:1 speaks about some "adversaries *[tsare]* of Judah and Benjamin." But why are they called "adversaries"? It is not clear. They appear to be friendly and supportive of the Jews and their building activities. They say: "Let us build with you; for we worship your God as you do, and we have been sacrificing to him ever since the days of Esarhaddon [680-669 B.C.E.] king of Assyria who brought us here" (v. 2). There is no reason to doubt this statement. Assyrian kings often transported people of a conquered country to another place in order to make revolt less likely. We do not have extrabiblical evidence for this particular action of Esarhaddon, but we know that his successor, Assurbanipal (668-627; called Osnappar in 4:10), continued the transportation of peoples during his reign. These people professed to worship the God of the Jews and to have been faithful in sacrificing to him since that time, that is, over one hundred years.

Their offer of help is bluntly refused. The Jews, headed by Zerubbabel and Joshua, respond that they, and they "alone" *(yahad)*, have been given the right to build by Cyrus (4:3). There is no discussion of the legitimacy of the words of these people (who appear to be predominantly, at least, non-Jews). But there must have been more to this exchange than is written down. We are only reading a summary of this confrontation that is provided by the author. There are a number of such summaries in the Bible. Recognizing these forms is important to sound and sensible preaching and teaching. For example, in Matt. 9:9 we are informed that Jesus "saw a man called Matthew sitting at the tax

28

office; and he said to him, 'Follow me.' And he rose and followed him." Jesus and Matthew had more to do with each other than that quick passing and the terse command. "Follow me" is a *focused summary* of their relationship. Because we are dealing with this kind of summary in Ezra 4:1-3 (and elsewhere in the book) the situation is unclear to us.

The "Adversaries" Are Non-Jews?

Who are these "adversaries"? Are they to be identified with the "peoples of the lands" (3:3) whom the Jews feared when they set up the altar? Most likely. The Jews held apart from them because they considered these people to be unacceptable before Yahweh. From the Jewish point of view, they may have "feared the LORD" but they "also served their own gods, after the manner of the nations from among whom they had been carried away" (2 Kgs. 17:33). Notice that in Ezra 6:21 we are informed that those who separated themselves "from the pollutions of the *peoples of the land* to worship the LORD, the God of Israel," were allowed to take part in the Passover celebration. If, therefore, these adversaries are to be identified with the "peoples of the lands," then it seems clear that they are non-Jews.

The "Adversaries" Are Jews?

Another designation for those who oppose the actions of the returned exiles occurs in 4:4: "the people of the land." These people for many years "discouraged the people of Judah, and made them afraid to build, and hired counselors against them to frustrate their purpose" (vv. 4-5). Although some scholars believe that "people of the land" is just another name for "peoples of the lands," it may be that they represent another opposition group made up of Jews. The name occurs rather often in the Bible, but it is not certain that it always refers to the same people. For example, in Hag. 2:4 the "people of the land" are included among the people of Yahweh who will raise a new temple (cf. also Zech. 7:5). In Ezra 4:4, however, "the people of the land" actively oppose the rebuilding project of the Jews. If the "people of the land" are seen as the basic native population of the land, in which there is some diversity, then one can account for this seeming contradiction. It is possible, then, that the "adversaries" in 4:1 are not foreigners but Jews. Due to the *summary character* of this material in 4:1-6, however, the identity of the "adversaries" may not be established with certainty.

JUMPING AHEAD OF THE STORY (4:6-23)

The author of the book of Ezra is writing about events (beginning ca. 538 B.C.E.) that took place long before his day (ca. 300 B.C.E.). As he writes about the various groups that caused the Jews trouble in the *rebuilding of the temple,* his mind seems to skip to other times of hardship, e.g., to the fierce resistance to the *rebuilding of the city and the city wall.* This "skip of the mind" appears to be an explanation for the inclusion of vv. 6-23 at this point in the narrative. This material relates to the building of the city walls during the rule of Xerxes (Ahasuerus), whose reign is dated 485-465 B.C.E., whereas the previous text (i.e., 4:1-5) had to do with the difficulties encountered while attempting to build the temple shortly after 539 B.C.E. Most likely, the author has not made a mistake in chronology; he has placed vv. 6-23 here because the theme is the same as that in vv. 1-5, namely, opposition. For commentary on opposition to the rebuilding of the city walls, see our commentary on Nehemiah in this volume.

BACK TO THE REBUILDING OF THE TEMPLE (4:24)

Ezra 4:24, which informs us that work on the temple stopped, is the continuation of 4:1-5. The opposition was so strong (4:1-5) that it brought the project to a standstill.

Is Opposition to the Rebuilding of the Temple Wrong?

Why did some people oppose the rebuilding of the temple? No reasons are given. But those who oppose this project are depicted as people who are opposed to the Jews *and* to God. This view of the conflict may, in fact, be the true representation of the situation, but the matter may not be as simple as it first appears.

The book of Ezra is not the only place in the Bible where we read about opposition to the temple. As early as the time of David there was concern about the construction of a temple in Jerusalem. Some people believed that a temple was inappropriate for a God who was known to be One who *walked* with his people (2 Sam. 7:4-11).

A temple *can be* a very dangerous structure. Although the temple, its personnel, and its ritual may nourish a community, as the book of Psalms demonstrates, the temptation is strong to identify God's presence too closely with the temple building and ritual. After the first temple was built in Israel, the prophets did not advocate that it be torn down or set aside; they did, however, direct threatening words against those who loved the temple too much. They stood over against those who placed their trust in the temple and its ritual and forgot the character of him to whom the temple witnessed (cf. Jer. 7:1-15).

What can be good can also become bad. There is no lack of examples of this potential in ancient and modern history. Too often, these examples are found in the areas of religion. Religion (whether Jewish, Christian, or some other faith) has frequently become so programmed by ritual, doctrine, and administrative procedure that it loses the dynamism of its beginnings. In an attempt to capture God, it ends up with the worship of an idol — and becomes oppressive.

THE TEMPLE: AN OLD CONFLICT RENEWED

Conflict over the temple was an old issue in Israel; after the Exile it became an explosive question once again. The following survey of opinions concerning the temple will provide a context in which we can better evaluate the place of the temple in Ezra and Nehemiah.

Ezekiel: Yes, Build the Temple

The controversy about a temple building is very old, as we have noted above. During the Exile and the postexilic period, the temple became a controversial issue once more. Ezekiel (ca. 593-570), represented the thoughts of many Jews in exile when he envisaged a restored Israel whose center was the temple.

In this temple community the Zadokite priests were the ruling body. The Levites, viewed by Ezekiel as a group that "went astray" (44:9-14), occupy a secondary role within the temple; probably for this reason were so few Levites among the people that returned to the land (Ezra 2:40; 8:15). The inner court of the temple was reserved for the priests and Levites (44:17); the general Jewish population was limited to the outer court (Ezek. 44:19). Even the "prince" *(nasi)*, the Davidic ruler, was restricted in his movements (Ezek. 46:1-10). When the priests and Levites moved from the inner court to the outer court, where the people congregated, they had to remove their sacred vestments "lest they communicate holiness to the people with their garments" (Ezek. 44:19). The central point of Ezek. 40–48 is clear: *the temple is the place of God's presence.* From it flows blessing to the whole land (Ezek. 47:1-12).

Haggai and Zechariah: Yes, Build the Temple

When the Jews returned to the land, Haggai and Zechariah (and later Ezra and Nehemiah) carried forward the program of Ezekiel. Haggai announced that the hard times which the newly returned Jews experienced were due to the fact that the temple had not been rebuilt (Hag. 1:2-11). The laying of the temple foundation, the prophet declares, would bring blessing to the community (Hag. 2:18-19). The argument of Haggai, observes Robert Carroll (*When Prophecy Failed*, 159-60), is basically that of Amos: curse and blessing are brought about by Yahweh (Amos 4:6-11). However, "ironically Amos's critique had been directed against a people all too willing to attend to the sanctuary and to off-load gifts and sacrifices on to the deity, whereas Haggai's complaint was that they ignored the sanctuary yet expected to prosper." In Amos (and other preexilic prophets), Yahweh brings, or will bring, ruin because the people are too much concerned about temple matters; in Haggai, Yahweh brings trouble because too little attention is given to the temple.

Isaiah 56 — 66: Opposition to the Temple

The argument of Haggai illustrates how far Israel has "moved along" in her thinking. At one time, Yahweh indicated that he did not really care for a temple, because he was a walking God. He preferred to be with his people wherever they journeyed (2 Sam. 7:4-11). Now, Haggai interprets Yahweh to be saying that the temple is necessary to his saving presence in the land.

Haggai's oracle presents no surprise because for centuries the temple had been the central focus of God's presence, but there is evidence that some other people had memory of the old traditions with regard to the temple. The "temple thinking" of Ezekiel, Haggai, and Zechariah was opposed by the circle of Jews who preserved the prophetic oracles of Isa. 56 — 66. They believed that the program presented in the oracles of the above prophets placed too much importance on the temple and too little on what was central to faith. In his attack on the temple in Acts 7:47-50, Stephen quoted Isa. 66:1-2:

> Thus says the LORD:
>   "Heaven is my throne
> and the earth is my footstool;
> what is the house which you would build for me,
>   and what is the place of my rest? . . .
> But this is the man to whom I will look,
>   he that is humble and contrite of spirit,
>   and trembles at my word."

Opposition to the Temple Brings Persecution

But this community of believers in Yahweh, who protest the exaggerated importance given the temple, who resist the exclusivism of the program outlined in Ezek. 40 – 48, are expelled from the faith community. The ruling faction of the Jewish community (the Zadokites?) does not recognize them as part of Israel — as part of Abraham (Isa. 63:16). But Yahweh recognizes them and threatens punishment upon those who have cast them out. The threat is directed to "temple people"; *they* are now Yahweh's "enemies," according to the interpretation of the author of Isa. 66:5-6:

> Hear the word of the LORD,
>   you who tremble at his word:
> "Your brethren who hate you
>   and cast you out for my name's sake
> have said, 'Let the LORD be glorified,
>   that we may see your joy';
> but it is they who shall be put to shame."
> "Hark, an uproar from the city!
>   A voice from the temple!
> The voice of the LORD,
>   rendering recompense to his enemies!"

Isaiah 56 – 66: Foreigners Welcome

The viewpoint of the Isaian community (Isa. 56 – 66) stood at a great distance from the viewpoint expressed by Ezekiel and those who followed him — including Ezra and Nehemiah. In contrast to the restrictive program proposed by Ezek. 40 – 48, the Isaian community believes that Yahweh welcomes foreigners to his temple.

> And the foreigners who join themselves to the LORD
>   to minister to him, to love the name of the LORD,
>   and to be his servants,
> every one who keeps the sabbath, and does not profane it,
>   and holds fast my covenant — these I will bring to my
>   holy mountain,
>   and make them joyful in my house of prayer;
> their burnt offerings and their sacrifices
>   will be accepted on my altar;
> for my house shall be called a house of prayer
>   for all peoples. (Isa. 56:6-8)

Not only may foreigners join Yahweh's community, it appears that they will be welcomed into the priesthood (Isa. 66:21)! A full analysis of this material is impossible here, but for a further discussion of this controversy in the exilic and postexilic periods, see the influential book of Paul Hanson, *The Dawn of Apocalyptic*, 32-279; and the excellent summary and critique of this volume by Robert P. Carroll, "Twilight of Prophecy or Dawn of Apocalyptic?" *JSOT* 14 (1979): 3-35. In addition, consult the following helpful volumes on Isa. 56–66: G. A. F. Knight, *The New Israel: Isaiah 56–66* (a volume in the present series); and Elizabeth Achtemeier, *The Community and Message of Isaiah 56–66*.

Postexilic Judaism: Varied Views Concerning the Temple

The passages quoted above from Isa. 56–66 make us aware that some Jews in the postexilic period opposed a temple program that was being instituted. Although we are not furnished a detailed description of the kind of temple program *they* wanted, we are given a general idea of their concerns: they longed for a genuine piety (Isa. 66:2), an openness to other Jews (Isa. 66:5), and a welcome to every Gentile who loves Yahweh and "holds fast" to the covenant (Isa. 56:6). The caution made elsewhere in this commentary bears repeating: we know so little about the postexilic community (which means we miss the subtleties of encounter) that care must be taken not to exaggerate the divisions which are present (see, e.g., how older scholars have overstated the differences between Jesus and the Pharisees). Nevertheless, it seems true that *the views of Ezra and Nehemiah (and the editor/author who relates to us the story of their work) stood closer to the Ezekiel-Haggai-Zechariah temple program than to the community reflected in Isa. 56–66 that had reservations about the temple project.*

Almost every religious community knows the tension of exclusion and inclusion. On the one hand, to include people without distinction is dangerous because the very core of the community's life may be undercut by allowing people to enter who do not care about the basic beliefs or actions of the community. On the other hand, exclusion is also dangerous. *Communities given to exclusion frequently become harsh, "pinched" groups who continue to live long after they are dead.*

When to Say No; When to Say Yes

In spite of certain dangers, occasions do arise when a community may be forced to emphasize separation and restriction; when it does pursue such a policy (even for good reasons), however, it frequently suffers severe criticism. Psalm 1 is very offensive to some people because of its sharp, firm refusal to approve association with the wicked, the sinners, and the scoffers. *But the community that does not say no to ruinous people* (who set themselves against that which gives life to the group) *cannot hope to exist for long.* For all of us, yes is a more pleasant word than no. But the person or group that is unable to say no may also be the one whose yes has but little value.

Some individuals and communities, however, tend to say no before they even consider the possibility of yes. For example, Mark 9:38-41 tells of a man who went about casting out demons in the name of Jesus. The disciples come to Jesus and say: " 'Teacher . . . we forbade him, because he was not following us.' But Jesus said, 'Do not forbid him; for no one who does a mighty work in my name will be able soon after to speak evil of me. *For he that is not against us is for us*' " (see a similar story in Num. 11:26-30). Naturally, this kind of approach can be misused, as can the following negative statement: "He who is not with me is against me, and he who does not gather with me scatters" (Luke 11:23). But the presence of both kinds of statements in the Bible speaks a message to us that we might not fully hear if one of them were missing. If we decide that one of these statements appears to fit our situation, we are nevertheless reminded of the other truth that should at least be considered!

Ezra and Nehemiah: A Summary

As the above sayings of Jesus constitute a check on each other, so the two different views of the temple and its community (i.e., Ezekiel-Haggai-Zechariah-Ezra-Nehemiah versus Isa. 56 – 66) stand before us today for consideration. It is difficult at this late date to decide whether the leaders of the early Jewish returnees were too exclusive in their relationships to other groups in the land. From our viewpoint they seem to have been so. In terms of preserving a tradition and creating a future, however, they may have done what needed to be done. But the other tradition, advocated by the community that produced Isa. 56 – 66, was not silenced. If it did not influence significantly the leaders of the returnees, it did make itself known in later Jewish communities where Gentiles felt comfortable in Jewish synagogues and where proselytes were welcomed. Further, the Isa. 56 – 66 community continued to live on in Christianity, which in principle, at least, included male and female, Jew and Gentile, bond and free. Knowing the strength of this tradition in the history of Judaism and Christianity, we must listen to the Isaian community carefully when we read Ezra-Nehemiah so that we can hear the *full* word of God.

THE REBUILDING OF
THE TEMPLE
Ezra 5:1-17

WORK BEGINS AGAIN UNDER HAGGAI AND
ZECHARIAH (5:1-2)

In 4:1-5, the author speaks of the opposition that developed to
the temple-rebuilding activities. After a fairly lengthy parenthesis
which interrupts the chronology and the narrative concerning the
temple (4:6-23), we are informed that the resistance to work on
the temple was so strong that activity on this project was brought
to a standstill until the second year of Darius, king of Persia (ca.
520 B.C.E.; cf. 4:24). It was at this time that Haggai and Zechariah prophesied to the Jews who were in the land (Ezra 5:1; cf.
Hag. 1:1; Zech. 1:1). They call for the rebuilding of the temple
(Hag. 1:1-8; Zech. 1:16-17), and the people led by the Davidic
Zerubbabel and Joshua, the high priest, picked up the difficult
task of rebuilding "the house of God which is in Jerusalem" (Ezra
1:1-2; cf. Hag. 1:12-15).

There are some historical problems associated with the author's narrative concerning the foundations of the temple (e.g.,
the relationship of the work of Sheshbazzar to that of Zerubbabel;
cf. Ezra 3:8-10; 5:1-2; 5:16). It is possible that the author, writing
over one hundred years after some of the events, may have made
some chronological slips. Although discussion of this matter is
important, it should not be allowed to blur the focus of the author's intention. Our author is concerned about the establishment
of the temple community — a new beginning for Yahweh's people
in the land.

Haggai and Zechariah: A Call to Rebuild the Temple (5:1)

As indicated above, work on the temple stopped for a period of
time because of strong opposition to the rebuilding activity (4:1-5,
24). In the books of Haggai and Zechariah, however, there is no

mention of any opposition to the building of the temple. To Haggai the greatest obstacle was not opposition but the uncaring, uncommitted attitude of the Jews. This need not mean that Haggai was unaware of opposition to the temple project. There was, without doubt, hostility to this venture before and during the time of Haggai. But it may be that by the time of Darius, Haggai was convinced that it was no longer the hostile, outside community that was the obstacle to rebuilding; the obstruction was within the hearts of the Jews themselves. They were unwilling to make the effort.

Sometimes we excuse ourselves from accomplishing certain goals in life because our inner lack of commitment causes us to exaggerate the strength of the outside difficulties (see, e.g., Num. 13:30 – 14:12 and Luke 14:15-24). The altar had been rebuilt and many Jews had probably settled for worship at the temple "ruins."

Zerubbabel and Jeshua (5:2): Eschatological Figures in Haggai and Zechariah

We are fortunate in having two reports in the Bible concerning the appearance of Zerubbabel and Jeshua (also spelled Joshua). In the books of Haggai and Zechariah, these two leaders are "messianic" or "eschatological" figures. They are leaders in a new era that is about to break in on Israel. The temple is being rebuilt; it is the place where God is especially present with his people.

This temple makes a difference in the response of nature. Before the foundations of the temple were laid, the people suffered ruinous harvests; now, with the temple on its way to completion, the vine, the fig tree, and the olive tree all bring forth abundance (Hag. 2:18-19; cf. Hag. 1:5-11 and Zech. 8:11-12).

But the temple makes a difference in history also. God is about to "shake all nations, so that the treasures of all nations shall come in, and I will fill this house [i.e., the temple] with splendor, says the LORD of hosts" (Hag. 2:7; cf. Zech. 8:11-13).

Zerubbabel: A Temple Builder —and King?

Zerubbabel, the builder of the temple and a descendant from the family of David, is exalted, as we said above, as an "eschatological" ruler in Haggai and Zechariah. Although he is not called "king" or "prince," he is doing what has always been the responsibility of kings in Israel and in the ancient world, that is, building or rebuilding the temple (see, e.g., the temple activity of Solomon, Hezekiah, and Josiah; consult the article of Donna Runnalls, "The King as Temple Builder: A Messianic Typology," in *Spirit within Structure*, 15-26).

The oracle announced by Haggai concerning Zerubbabel is not one addressed to a second-level administrator; it has to do with a kingly figure: "On that day, says the LORD of hosts, I will take you, O Zerubbabel *my servant,* the son of Shealtiel, says the LORD, and make you a *signet ring;* for *I have chosen you,* says the LORD of hosts" (Hag. 2:23). Mountains become plains before Zerubbabel (Zech. 4:7). Joshua, the high priest, is also a figure of the end of days; he and Zerubbabel are the two "anointed [*bene-hayyitshar* — sons of oil] who stand by the LORD of the whole earth" (Zech. 4:14). Concerning the royal character of Zerubbabel, see further David Peterson, "Zerubbabel and Jerusalem Temple Reconstruction," *CBQ* 36 [1974]: 366-72). On the character of the message of Haggai and Zechariah, consult Carroll Stuhlmueller, *Haggai and Zechariah,* a commentary which will soon be published in this series.

Zerubbabel: Descended from David

The expectant mood which characterizes Haggai and Zechariah is surely due in part to the fact that Zerubbabel comes from the family of David and now has been appointed governor over the returned exiles. The old hopes expressed in the prophets and psalms concerning a Davidic ruler are awakened with his appearance. The lament in Ps. 89, which calls upon Yahweh to be true to his promise to David, must have echoed in the minds of many Jews. With the rise of Zerubbabel, these Jews must have thought: Perhaps *now* Yahweh will act to bring about the restoration of Davidic rule. This optimism was, no doubt, nourished by the expectation of a newly restored community which centers about the temple, the priests, and the Davidic prince (see Ezek. 40 – 48).

But this messianic outlook was fed not only by the rise of the Davidic Zerubbabel and the existence of Ezekiel's hopes; it was encouraged also by a political crisis in the Persian government. Darius I succeeded to kingship after the death of Cambyses, but not without struggle. For two years a civil war raged until Darius was finally able to establish himself as ruler. However, such a victory did not pacify immediately the whole empire. Fear and insecurity, as well as an expectation that something new was about to happen, remained for some time. The rise of Zerubbabel and Joshua in this kind of context led many Jews to believe that this chaotic period was the work of Yahweh — he was shaking the nations in preparation for a new era he was about to create through the leadership of Zerubbabel and Joshua (see Geo

Widengren, "The Persian Period," in *Israelite and Judaean History*, 520-22).

But the reinstitution of past forms (such as kingship) is frequently a futile hope. What was good and successful at one point in life may not be so at another. In the hymn "Once to Every Man and Nation," James Russell Lowell spoke the painful truth: "Ancient good [often] becomes uncouth." Jeremiah felt the sting of this truth and prophesied, correctly, that no descendant of the last king of Israel would ever sit on the throne of David (Jer. 22:30).

Hopes Unfulfilled

The great expectations concerning Zerubbabel were never realized. Following the time of Haggai and Zechariah, we hear no more of him. We have no hint of what happened to him. He is succeeded by Joshua (cf. Zech. 5:9-14 — note that the RSV translates "crown" but the MT has "crowns"), who may have been followed by other Zadokite leaders (e.g., Ezra). Zerubbabel may also have been succeeded by other governors selected from the family of David (see Paul Hanson, *Dawn of Apocalyptic*, 349), but we do not know this for certain. See, however, Ulrich Kellermann, *Nehemia*, 159, who has argued that Nehemiah is of Davidic descent. We will discuss this matter in our commentary on Nehemiah. But, whatever truth this supposition has, Zerubbabel's disappearance from history is a mystery. Whether he was removed by the Persians (because of revolutionary activity), lost out in the rivalry with Joshua and his priestly supporters, or simply died without fulfilling these hopes we do not know.

How does one deal with failure? *How does one get up when his hopes have let him down?* Israel faced that painful situation in the Exile itself. She had counted on the continuance of the Davidic monarchy, the temple, and Jerusalem, but they all faded away. The pain of that experience may be seen in the book of Lamentations and in Isa. 40:27. Now the returnees had to face failure once again. They had counted on Zerubbabel, but their hope rested on the wrong person.

Ezra and Nehemiah: A Revised View of Zerubbabel

The author of the book of Ezra is telling the story of the building of the temple from a perspective of one hundred years or more after the event. Zerubbabel and Joshua, he explains, had a leading role in raising up the structure; they were urged to do so, he says, by the prophets Haggai and Zechariah, who spoke "in the name of the God of Israel who was over them" (Ezra 5:1). Clearly, the writer of Ezra believes that the work of Zerubbabel and Joshua had the support of the prophets (they assisted them, 5:2), and that this work was inspired by God. But there is utter silence about the "messianic" hopes that rested upon them at one time (i.e., in the time of Haggai and Zechariah). The reader of Ezra becomes aware that there is a part of history missing; the writer does not share with us the immense hurt that some Jews must have experienced with the failure of the hopes set upon Zerubbabel and Joshua. Nowhere in Ezra-Nehemiah is there any *overt* "messianic" or "eschatological" mood or theme. For a helpful discussion of unfulfilled prophecy, see Robert Carroll, *When Prophecy Failed*, 157-84.

Did the author of Ezra and Nehemiah feel the pain of failure as sharply as did the early Jewish settlers? Perhaps the passage of time had healed the hurt somewhat. Or is it possible that the author took another view of Zerubbabel? In 1:1 he has indicated his awareness of Jeremiah's prophecies concerning the future (especially, probably, the seventy-year prophecy). Did he know and was he in full agreement with another prophecy that Jeremiah made about the future — the one in which the prophet declares that no descendant of King Jehoiachin would ever rule from the throne of David (Jer. 22:24-30)? Possibly. At least, it may be said that the passage of time has brought him to the recognition that Jeremiah was right and Haggai was wrong. This may explain why he can recognize Zerubbabel's contribution to the rebuilding of the temple but say nothing about the expectations that swirled about him during the time of Haggai and Zechariah.

Zerubbabel: Failure but also Success

One reason why the author of Ezra may not have been as disturbed by the unfulfilled oracles (concerning Zerubbabel) as we are is that he knew that an important portion of that prophecy *did take place*, that is, the temple was built by Zerubbabel. In Jewish tradition, the second temple is, in fact, identified as Zerubbabel's temple. For the author of Ezra and Nehemiah, the return of the people to the land and the rebuilding of the temple was a monumental achievement — an accomplishment that was of far greater importance than the rule of Zerubbabel. Often, however, the modern reader fails to appreciate this point of view. Instead of emphasizing the positive (i.e., what did happen), the focus is on the negative (what did not happen).

THE PERSIAN GOVERNMENT INVESTIGATES THE TEMPLE PROJECT (5:3-17)

Representatives of the Persian government became aware of the temple-building project and decided to investigate. This investigation may have come about through the efforts of the "people of the land" who informed the government of this project (Ezra 4:4-5). If, at this time, Darius was still attempting to establish himself as ruler after putting down a rival, then he and his officials would be very concerned about any unusual activity going on among a subject people. This would be especially true if they had heard rumors that this rebuilt temple was considered to be the center of a nationalistic movement — a movement that would "shake all nations" (Hag. 2:7).

The Persian officials wanted to know the names of the people working on the project (Ezra 5:4). These names were given to them and were recorded (5:10). The legal and political importance of the list in Ezra 2 and Neh. 7 now becomes clear. The officials also asked the name of the one who granted them permission to build (Ezra 5:3). The Jews responded by referring to the decree of Cyrus (5:13, 17). The officials took the information and sent a letter to Darius to validate the information given, especially the response of the Jews concerning the decree of Cyrus (5:17). The officials themselves demonstrate no hostility to the Jews.

The Eye of God Watching over His Own (5:5)

While awaiting a reply from the Persian government, the officials allowed the Jews to continue working on the temple. This was taken as a sign of a special intervention on the part of God: "But the eye of their God was upon the elders of the Jews." The Bible witnesses often to God's intervention in the affairs of history. The OT is a centuries-long story of God working in the life of the Israelite community to bring about his will in the world. Together with other biblical writers, Ezra and Nehemiah testify to God's favorable action on behalf of his people (e.g., Ezra 1:1; 8:31; Neh. 4:15; 9:7-15). This belief stands at the center of the community of faith.

God's Eye on Us: What Does It Mean?

How should we understand the above phrase? One response would be to say that we should understand it as a true statement. Few readers would wish to dispute that response, but that affirmation

41

does not help our understanding very much. The interpreter must be careful not to denigrate this witness, but neither should it be exaggerated. There are those who do not believe that God has much (if anything) to do with our world. But the Bible knows of those who *exaggerate the activity of God in history* and thereby misrepresent his relationship to the world. For example, the friends of Job wanted to affirm that God always protects his own people and punishes those who oppose him (Job 4:7-11). Job knows that this view of God and the world is wrong (Job 21:1-26), and, according to the author of that book, God agrees with him (Job 42:7-9).

Is God Always in Control?

Life does not always happen the way it should happen, nor, perhaps, the way God prefers it to happen. We must not take this statement concerning the "eye" of God, quoted above, and make it a universal declaration about how God takes care of his own — all the time — everywhere. At times there seems to be no "eye" watching over people of faith who are in great need. This tragic truth is supported by an endless list of people who have been persecuted, tortured, and killed with no noticeable movement by God: pious believers who died in the persecutions of Antiochus Epiphanes, early Jewish and Christian martyrs of Roman times and later, the many Jews who suffered Christian suppression, the devout and poor of every age, the blacks and other minority groups, the Jews murdered in the Nazi Holocaust.

It is this painful truth about life that lies in back of the laments offered to God in the OT. The person offering the lament believes in God with his whole heart. He knows that God has helped others, but he also knows that God has not helped him. In handling the matter of the "eye of their God" in 5:5, one may find the psalms of lament helpful guides in interpretation. Sometimes we perceive that God intervenes to rescue and help us, sometimes not. This is a truth recognized by the psalms of lament — but a truth that resists being structured into some theological doctrine.

The author of Ezra 5 is writing from the vantage point of more than one hundred years after the rebuilding of the temple. He must have known of the many hardships that had come upon the returned exiles (e.g., the fierce opposition which hindered the rebuilding of the temple and the city wall). But the author also knew that in the midst of many hardships, some things went well. These times (and the good fortune recorded in Ezra 5:5 is *one* of these times) he mentions as something for which God should be praised.

Servants of God (5:11)

This is the only time in the book of Ezra where the Jews represent themselves as the "servants" of God (cf. 9:11, where the prophets are thus designated). Although Israel is often called "the servant of God," we should not read that emphasis too quickly into this reference. (See our comments on Israel as "servant" in the commentary on Neh. 1:4-11.) Here in v. 11 the term "servants" has another level of meaning. This statement does not seem to emphasize the peculiar character of the Jews as a covenant people; rather it is a statement that attempts to establish a relationship between the Jews and the Persians. According to the Persian governor's report to Darius, the Jews say: "We are the servants of the God of heaven and earth." Tattenai, the Persian governor, is probably representing accurately what the Jews actually said. Why did not the Jews say that they were the servants of *Yahweh?* Most likely because they did not wish to appear "different" to the Persians. The statement that *was* made by the Jews would be understood by the Persians in somewhat the following fashion: "We, *like you,* are servants of the God of heaven and earth." In other words, it was a reply that would not offend the Persian officials. *The use of tact is not a sign of weakness. One need not offend others in order to be faithful* (1 Cor. 10:23-33).

THE TEMPLE BUILT: DIVINE-
HUMAN PARTNERSHIP
Ezra 6:1-22

THE SURPRISING RESPONSE OF DARIUS (6:1-12)

Sometimes one receives more than one could ever hope for. Challenged by the Persian officials about the validity of their building program (5:3-4), the Jews could only hope that the documents and other information that they gave them (5:6-16) would result in permission to continue the rebuilding of the temple. That anxious hope was fulfilled. The search uncovered the decree of Cyrus, which legitimated the activities of the Jews (6:1-5). Darius issues an order that the Persian officials are to "keep away" and to "let the work on this house of God alone" (vv. 6-7). But, in addition to this welcome reaffirmation of their right to rebuild the temple, there was further good news.

With surprising generosity Darius decrees that the expense involved in the rebuilding activities be paid for from royal funds (6:8; cf. v. 4). Also, the king ordered the government to pay for the cost of burnt offerings made to "the God of heaven" (6:9-10). Threatening words are directed to those who would alter the king's decree in any manner and who would "destroy this house of God which is in Jerusalem" (6:11-12). What an incredible relief to a people anxiously awaiting the reply of Darius and fearing the worst!

Enlightened Self-Interest

As is true of so many "considerate" human responses, the decree of Darius does not grow out of pure generosity but rather from enlightened self-interest. The Persians knew that a benevolent government policy would help to create good will in troublesome areas of the kingdom and would therefore undercut revolutionary movements. During this period of his rule (i.e., the time of Haggai-Zechariah, ca. 520 B.C.E.), revolt endangered various parts

44

of the empire. The full support that the Persian king gave to the Jewish cult was a small price to pay for keeping the peace of the empire. What he did for the Jews, he did for other peoples in his kingdom and — no doubt — for the same reason.

Praying for Persian Royalty (6:10)

In return for his support of the Jewish community, Darius expects the community to pray for him and his sons before "the God of heaven" (6:10). The use of this title (discussed in ch. 1) created Persian good will toward the Jews because it was a non-particular title. The ambiguity of this title enabled the Jews to talk to and cooperate with the Persians while maintaining the integrity of their own faith in Yahweh.

In 5:11-12 we noted that the Jews used titles for God that would not be offensive to the Persians. Now 6:10 records a call for another accommodating action: in the holy temple, prayers are to be offered to God for Persian royalty. There is no reason to doubt that the request of the Persian king was granted.

The Jewish returnees were a people who placed great value on purity and separation, but they were not so religious that common sense failed them. To offend the Persian king by refusing to pray for him would doom the larger good, that is, the success of the rebuilding project and the survival of Jewish belief and practice. Minority groups, especially, come face to face with this kind of trade-off again and again. Sometimes accommodation can be made, sometimes not. When adjustment destroys the inner core of a community, then the community must say no. Surely, some Jews must have opposed prayers for the Persian emperor because for them it had the smell of collaboration.

Other Examples of Friendliness to Foreigners

There are, however, antecedents to the cooperative policy of the Jews during the Persian period. A number of OT narratives depict Israelites maintaining friendly relationships with those who have very different beliefs. Melchizedek, a non-Hebrew priest-king of Salem (Jerusalem), bestows a blessing upon Abraham, who responds by giving him a tithe of everything (Gen. 14:18-21). Further, the patriarch prays to God for Abimelech (Gen. 20:17), and he moves without major conflict among the Hittites (Gen. 23). Joseph gets on well in the court of Pharaoh; his father, Jacob, develops such a close relationship to the Egyptian ruler that he blesses Pharaoh (Gen. 47:10). A pious and wise people learn to get along with others as much as possible — and if the "others" are powerful that may be an additional incentive for peaceful relationships. Proverbs 20:2 cautions against provoking a king to anger, because death will be the result of that kind of foolish action. The Jewish community would not likely provoke the Persian king to anger by refusing what was, probably, a common request by the king of all subject peoples.

Adjusting to the Structures of Society

Jews have had to live as a minority group for ages. While in the main holding to their own traditions, they have also developed the policy of not offending the Gentiles. In part this policy was adopted out of sensitivity for the feelings of others. But it also reflects the desire of a minority group to live among others with as little conflict as possible.

Early Christians also sought the good will of those who stood outside the Christian community, not only because that attitude represented the character of the community of Christ, but also because the church did not wish to cause unnecessary troubles for itself in the larger society. As much as it was possible (i.e., without sacrificing the core of the church's life), Christians were urged to obey and cooperate with rulers who were over them (Rom. 13:1-7; 1 Pet. 2:13-17). However, the Bible itself describes times when the community of faith must not obey rulers if it is to retain the integrity of its traditions. In certain situations the only possible response is: "We must obey God rather than men" (Acts 5:29). These times are reflected in the books of Daniel and Revelation. In these situations, contrary to Paul's statement in another context, the ruler really *is* a "terror to good conduct" (Rom. 13:3) and must be opposed.

The Question: To Cooperate or to Oppose?

When to cooperate and when to oppose government (or the outside world generally) is not an easy decision to make. In the Maccabean period, some Jews cooperated with the oppressing monarch and in the process laid aside their faith. Likewise, some Christians sought the good will of the Roman government, but the "good will" was purchased at the expense of the integrity of faith. During Hitler's rule, many Christians took as their guide Paul's words that one should obey rulers because they are ordained of God (Rom. 13:1-2). But, in this case, obedience to the ruler really amounted to collaboration with evil against the rule of God. Each generation must face the question of the relationship of the faith community to the wider world and to government. The words and actions recorded in Ezra or in Paul's epistles can no more serve as universal, invariable models than can the writings in the books of Daniel or Revelation. But a community is given significant guidance as it listens to the conversation going on among these diverse writings and genuinely seeks to live out Torah and gospel in its life.

THE TEMPLE IS COMPLETED (6:13-15)

Confronted with the decree of Cyrus and the pronouncement of Darius, the opposition collapses. Finally, work moves swiftly forward, and in the year 515 B.C.E. the temple is finished. Verses 13-14 summarize the contributions of various persons to the project: the Persian officials (Tattenai and Shethar-bozenai) gave support to the building project as the king had commanded (vv. 6-10); Haggai and Zechariah prophesied (giving counsel and encouragement); and "the elders of the Jews built and prospered." The building was completed "by command of the God of Israel and by decree of Cyrus and Darius and Artaxerxes king of Persia." The words "command" and "decree" in the above quotation are translations of the same Aramaic root.

"By Command of God . . . and by Decree of Cyrus" (6:14)

The practical mindset of the biblical author is illustrated in these verses; the completion of the temple is made possible by a double decree — one issued by God and the other by Cyrus! This does not imply that God and Cyrus are equals. But the author knows that, in practical terms, God cannot bring about the building of the temple all by himself. There must be people to build, and, in this case, permission and support from the king is needed before God's decree can be accomplished. The writer has already told us that God "stirred up the spirit of Cyrus" (1:1) to issue the decree, so we know that behind the decree of Cyrus he sees Yahweh at work. But he does not press this thought continually upon the reader. He speaks according to the way it happened. *As a matter of fact*, the temple was built through the prophesying of Haggai and Zechariah, the work of the elders, and also by the command of God — and that of Cyrus.

Give People Credit!?

Sometimes our religious language masks the part that people play in accomplishing the will of God. We tend to downplay the contribution of people and to emphasize what God does. From one point of view this is exactly where the emphasis should fall, because all human activity ultimately depends on God. But from another point of view, failure to underscore human participation in achieving the divine purpose in life leads to a misunderstanding of the the relationship between God and people. Abraham Heschel declares, in concert with all people of faith, that humankind needs God; he is the source of all our life and activity. But Heschel goes further and says that *God needs us* also (*Man Is Not Alone: A Philosophy of Religion*, 241-51). At first sight it seems to be a shocking statement; is it possible that the Lord of the universe needs us?

We tend to reject such a thought because it seems to denigrate the power and majesty of the Creator. But the creation stories in the first chapters of Genesis help us to understand what Heschel is talking about. God creates humankind out of love, but also out of need. God is able to create the world and everything in it, but he "cannot" till the land and domesticate the animals; these kinds of tasks (and others, e.g., feeding the poor, healing the sick, building bridges and hospitals) he has given to his creatures.

If we move away from theological language for a moment and simply examine how things get done in this world, it is clear that God needs us; in fact, he depends on us. God may have need of human beings at other levels also, but in the practical flow of life, human beings are indispensable. The temple would not have been built if it had not been for Cyrus, Darius, the elders, Haggai, Zechariah, Sheshbazzar, Jeshua, and Zerubabbel. God needed them and therefore he "stirred" them to activity.

Zerubbabel and Jeshua Missing; Artaxerxes Added

In the list of people who are remembered for their part in the rebuilding of the temple, Zerubbabel and Jeshua are missing, even though Ezra 3:8-10 and passages in Haggai and Zechariah identify them as having played a prominent role in laying the foundation. This is ironic because later Jewish tradition remembers this sanctuary as Zerubbabel's temple!

The problem relating to the mention of Artaxerxes I (465-424) in v. 14 is the opposite of that concerning Zerubbabel and Jeshua. Zerubbabel and Jeshua are not mentioned but should have been; Artaxerxes is listed but should not have been. This Persian ruler had nothing to do with this early rebuilding project, which was completed fifty years before his rule.

Artaxerxes may have been mentioned because he supported additional work done on the temple. Jacob Myers (*Ezra. Nehemiah*,

53) suggests another possibility. He observes that this Persian ruler may have been associated with Nehemiah's work on the wall around the city — a project that was related to the temple in the mind of the author. His inclusion, then, among those responsible for the erection of the temple may be due to some thought associations that linked the building of the temple to the building of the city wall. While writing of the temple-building project and the contributions of Cyrus and Darius, his mind jumps from that time, that project, and those kings to a much later time — the time of Artaxerxes I. This compacting of time is not an unusual happening. Most of us have probably had the experience of speaking about one event and before we know it we are speaking about another related happening that took place at another time.

THE DEDICATION OF THE NEW TEMPLE (6:16-18)

What Could Never Happen, Happened (6:16)

Unexpected events happen; there are miraculous turnarounds in life. A people who thought themselves dead (Ezek. 37:1-10), forsaken (Isa. 40:27), doomed to live forever in an alien land, now stand before the temple which is built on the sacred site of the first temple. What has been destroyed has risen again; what was dreamed about has become reality. The joy of the returned exiles at the completion of the temple is the joy that springs up in those who, risking everything, achieve the impossible dream.

Costly Gifts from a Thankful Heart (6:17)

Let those who have been delivered from trouble by Yahweh, says the psalmist, "offer sacrifices of thanksgiving, and tell of his deeds in songs of joy" (Ps. 107:22; cf. 27:6). Many animals — at great cost to this poor community — are offered up to God: "one hundred bulls, two hundred rams, four hundred lambs . . . twelve he-goats" (v. 17). These sacrifices do not compare to the number offered when Solomon's temple was dedicated (cf. 1 Kgs. 8:63: "twenty-two thousand oxen and a hundred and twenty thousand sheep"), but for a small and poor community it represented a considerable gift.

Although the Bible reminds us that God values sincerity of heart in the offerer more than the number or value of the sacrifices (e.g., Mic. 6:6-8), David's words to Araunah should not pass without thought: "I will not offer burnt offerings to the LORD my God which cost me nothing" (2 Sam. 24:24). It is probably true that offerings which do not touch the pocketbook of the worshiper do not touch the heart either. Although Jewish and Christian congregations no longer offer animal or meal sacrifices, they are pressured by the same temptations, that is, to slide by with words and acts that cost the worshiper nothing.

Sorrow for Sin

A sin offering at the time of the dedication of the temple strikes the right note. The ritual speaks of sincere sorrow for wrongs done *and* of an earnest commitment to follow Yahweh (see Lev. 4 for a description of the sin-offering ritual). We should not imagine, as some have, that this offering was absolutely necessary so that the Jews could rid themselves of some seventy years of sin (i.e., from 587 B.C.E., when the temple was destroyed, to 515 B.C.E, when it was rebuilt). God does not *need* sacrifice in order to grant forgiveness; the Israelites do not *need* to sacrifice in order to be forgiven. God forgives those who seek him with a sincere heart (Ps. 51:17; 50:22-23). Sacrifices, like Christian baptism and the Lord's Supper, are symbolic actions that speak of the desire of the individual and the community.

The people of Israel lived without the temple and sacrifices from 587 to 515 B.C.E.; also from 70 C.E. to the present Jews have survived without a temple. Sacrifice was a traditional way in which to express one's love and commitment to God; it was a ritual that Israel shared with other peoples of the ancient world. Thus it is no surprise that, on returning to the land, the people erected a temple and, once more, instituted sacrificial rituals.

The twelve he-goats sacrificed in the sin offering are for "all Israel" (cf. Num. 7). Here and elsewhere (Ezra 2:2 par. Neh. 7:7 and Ezra 8:35) the hope is expressed that the restoration of all Israel will be the result of the beginnings made under Haggai's and Zechariah's leadership. Herbert Ryle's comments are to the point: "The remnant who had returned make solemn confession of sin in the name of the whole scattered and dispersed race. They acknowledge the essential unity of Israel's tribes alike in the consequences of sin, in the possibilities of restoration, and in the renewed consecration to God's service" (*Ezra and Nehemiah*, 83).

THE PASSOVER (6:19-22)

After years of hardship, poverty, and determined opposition, the temple is rebuilt and the traditional worship rituals are observed. The feasts of Passover and Unleavened Bread are now celebrated.

The Passover, especially, pointed to the event that created Israel: Yahweh's rescue of his people from the abuse of Egypt (Exod. 12:1-27).

The Exodus happened in the past; it is not, however, a past event, because the God of the Exodus continues to exercise his power and grace in the life of the Israelite community. The Exodus is a continuing event. In the Passover celebration the worshiper not only looks back on the past but also experiences it as a present reality (see Helmer Ringgren, *Sacrifice in the Bible,* 43-50; and Robert Daly, *The Origins of the Christian Doctrine of Sacrifice,* 38-41). The following passage from the Mishnah (quoted by Daly in the above volume, p. 41) must reflect in essence what early Israelites thought when they celebrated the Passover. The praise given to God in the last two sentences testifies to the present reality of the Exodus for those who live hundreds of years after this marvelous saving event.

> In all generations it is the duty of a man to consider himself as if he had come forth from Egypt; as Scripture says, "And thou shall relate unto thy son in that day saying, 'Because of this hath the Eternal wrought for me when I came forth from Egypt.' Therefore we are in duty bound to give thanks, to praise, to laud, to glorify, to exalt, to honour, to bless, to extol and to adore Him Who performed for our forefathers and for us all these miracles; He brought us forth from slavery to freedom, from sorrow to rejoicing, from mourning to festivity, from darkness to light, and from servitude to redemption; and let us say before Him, 'Praise ye the Eternal.' " (*Pesahim* 10:5, in *Mishnayoth,* trans. and ed. by Philip Blackman, 2:219).

Exodus and Resurrection

The past and present reality of the Exodus may be appreciated by Christians if the Exodus event is compared to the resurrection of Christ. The resurrection is an event of the past, but it is also a contemporary one in which Christians today participate. Experiencing the Exodus (or the Resurrection) as a present event gives one confidence concerning the future. The God who has initiated this salvation act will bring it to completion (cf. Phil. 1:6); he will not allow the future to write "void" over it.

"So They Killed the Passover Lamb" (6:20)

The above sentence creates different images for Jews and Christians. Jews are reminded of the Exodus event (Exod. 12:1-27); to Christians, however, though there is an awareness of the Exodus context, the "Passover lamb" points most powerfully to the figure of Jesus. Paul states the relationship most clearly: "For Christ, our paschal lamb, has been sacrificed" (1 Cor. 5:7). This statement is not a formal theological declaration; it arises, as do so many of Paul's statements about Christ, out of a practical, ethical issue. That Paul could use it as a part of an illustration indicates that this analogy was well known in early Christianity.

Explaining the New in Terms of the Old

All of us tend to explain what is new in terms of what is old — in terms of what is familiar to us. Past experience gives understanding to new experience. For example, the new leader, Joshua, is understood in terms of the old leader, Moses (Josh. 1:1-4); deliverance from Babylon and the resettlement of the land is understood as a new exodus, a new creation, and a new conquest (see Isa. 40–55). Ezekiel understands the future in terms of the old temple community that he knows and loves (Ezek. 40–48).

NT writers continued the Israelite tradition of understanding the new in the light of the old (see Roger Le Déaut, *La Nuit Pascale*, 307-38). Thus, for example, Jesus is compared to:

    Adam (1 Cor. 15:45; Rom. 5:12-15)
    Moses (Acts 3:19-23)
    The Manna (John 6:31-38)
    The Bronze Serpent (John 3:14)
    The High Priest (Heb. 4:14)
    The Rolling Stone (1 Cor. 10:4)

When Paul identifies Jesus as the "paschal lamb" which "has been sacrificed" (1 Cor. 5:7), he is only doing what both OT and other NT writers have done — attempting to explain the new in terms of the old.

One must not press these correspondences too heavily. The NT authors who employ these analogies are attempting to answer the question: "Who is Jesus?" The question is answered not in terms of philosophical propositions, but by comparing Jesus to what was significant and well known in the Hebrew and Jewish tradition. Sometimes in pursuing this approach a NT writer contradicts logic. For example, Hebrews declares that Jesus is the perfect priest (4:14 – 5:10) and also the perfect sacrifice (9:11-28) which the perfect priest (i.e., Jesus) will offer to God. The writer to the Hebrews surely recognized this contradiction but it did not bother him. He spoke about correspondences, not about logic. By use of these analogies the Christian community is attempting to understand and communicate who Jesus *really* is. Many analogies are used because no one correspondence can fully explain the character and significance of Jesus Christ.

Jesus: The Paschal Lamb

The Passover tradition provided rich imagery for communicating the identity of Jesus. This is especially true of the Passover lamb, which attracted the attention of the NT writers. In addition to explicit references (1 Cor. 5:7; cf. 1 Pet. 1:18-19), there are allusions to this sacrificial lamb in the Gospels. For example, John 19:14, 31 set the death of Jesus at the time of the slaughtering of the Passover lamb. According to Exod. 12:46, no bones were to be broken on the lamb offered at Passover (cf. Num. 9:12). John 19:36, commenting on the death of Jesus, declares: "For these things took place that the scripture might be fulfilled, 'Not a bone of him shall be broken' " (see further Robert Daly, *The Origins of the Christian Doctrine of Sacrifice,* 41).

The Passover: Jewish and Christian Traditions

Although in Christianity the development of the Passover tradition differs considerably from the Israelite-Jewish tradition, there are basic similarities. In both: (1) the "Passover" speaks of the saving presence of God; (2) the death of the "spotless lamb" (i.e., the shedding of blood) is a means of life for those who belong to the community; (3) community ties are strengthened by the eating of the body; (4) the "Passover" celebrates a past event which is also a present reality; (5) confidence is created concerning the future because God has overcome the "enemy." For a further discussion of the Passover tradition in the OT, postbiblical Jewish literature, and the NT, see Notker Füglister, "Passover," in *Sacramentum Mundi,* 4:352-57.

The Passover: Outsiders Welcome (6:20-21)

At the completion of the temple, the returned Jews observe the Passover, which celebrates the event (i.e., the Exodus) which created Israel and is the continuing promise of Israel's future. But some outsiders were also included in the Passover meal, namely, "every one who had joined them and separated himself from the pollutions of the peoples of the land *[goye-ha'arets]* to worship the LORD, the God of Israel."

The above phrase, "peoples of the land" *(goye-ha'arets;* elsewhere also *'amme-ha'aretz)* is sometimes thought to be associated with another one, that is, "people of the land" *('am-ha'arets;* cf.

Ezra 4:4). They do not, however, refer to the same people. "People of the land" (singular) points to Jews who have remained in the land during the exilic period. "Peoples of the land" identifies foreigners (Gentiles), most of whom settled in the land after the fall of Jerusalem in 587. They are to be identified with those who are called the "peoples of the lands" (*'amme-ha'aratsoth;* cf. Ezra 9:1, 11).

A Yes to Outsiders

Who are these people that separated themselves from the "peoples of the land" to worship Yahweh and to eat the Passover meal? We have no certain information. They may have been Jews who had "gone over" to the practices of the foreign population (cf. 9:1, 11), but decided finally to return to Yahweh. It is also possible that they are non-Israelites who were attracted to this new Jewish community and resolved to become a part of it. We know that in the later times, many non-Jews were drawn to the Jewish synagogues — some even converting to Judaism.

Whatever the situation, whether it concerned Jews who were welcomed back into the covenant community or Gentiles who converted, the chapter ends with a yes to some people who had been standing on the outside and who wanted now to be on the inside. Why would people on the outside seek entrance to this community which was struggling to make its way in a hostile environment? To ask this question is to become aware of the attractive character of the society being formed by the returning exiles. Today, we look back on what these Jews did and, in view of later developments, are critical of it. However, *every society should be viewed in terms of its own time.* As the ancient Israelites brought a new kind of societal structure into the land in the time of Joshua (see John Hamlin, *Inheriting the Land: Joshua,* xvi-xx), so may the returning exiles have done in the postexilic period. In any case, for some people the way of life among the Jewish exiles was preferable to the way they had been living; they saw something in this community that meant "life" to them.

EZRA ARRIVES WITH TORAH
Ezra 7:1-28

EZRA: PRIEST AND SCRIBE (7:1-10)

Chapter 6 ended with the celebration over the rebuilt temple, which was completed under the reign of Darius in 515 B.C.E. With three words ("Now after this," v. 1), the author covers more than half a century and possibly more than a century of history. He introduces Ezra, who leads a group of exiles from Babylon to Palestine during the "seventh year of King Artaxerxes." If this ruler is Artaxerxes I, the date would be 458 B.C.E., but if he is identified as Artaxerxes II, the time indicated is 398 B.C.E.

Once again we become aware that the author's purpose is not to give us historical information. His focus is on Ezra, the teacher of Torah; he skips over a long period of time in order to introduce him. But even with regard to Ezra, we are given only a minimum of information. For example, the author gives us no information about Ezra's life in Babylon, and he offers no reason as to why Ezra did not come earlier. Presenting a full history of this period is not his intention.

Ezra: A Zadokite Priest (7:1-5)

The genealogy in 7:1-5 traces Ezra's priestly descendants back through Zadok to Aaron. Ezra is a Zadokite priest; he belongs to the priestly family that Ezekiel favored highly (Ezek. 44:15-16). His priestly status is mentioned in the decree of Artaxerxes (7:11, 12, 21). Ezra's standing as a Zadokite priest helps us understand, in part, his role as leader in the Jewish community (see our discussion on the temple in ch. 4).

Ezra: The Scribe (7:6)

In addition to the title "priest," Ezra is given the title of "scribe" *(sopher),* a title that may have had political as well as religious overtones. This title may refer to an administrative position that

Ezra held under the Persians (i.e., Administrator of Jewish Affairs). But this term appears also to identify Ezra as one who gives authoritative interpretation of Torah (7:10). This title (i.e., "scribe") was probably used in the exilic period as a description of the activity of Jewish priests in Babylon. They were unable to perform many of their priestly functions because no temple existed there, but they *were able* to continue their ancient role as interpreters of Torah (cf. Deut. 33:8-9; see Jacob Myers, "Scribe," in *IDB*, 4:246). If this was the situation, then the Persians quite likely appointed Ezra to the position of Scribe (i.e., a consultant on or an administrator of Jewish affairs for the Persians) because he was recognized in the community as an expert in Jewish tradition (i.e., he was "skilled in the law of Moses," v. 6).

Ezra and the Law of Moses (7:6, 10)

The references in Ezra to the "law of Moses" (7:6), the "law of the LORD" (7:10), and the "book of Moses" (6:18) point to the Pentateuch in a form close to which we have it now (so Jacob Myers, *Ezra. Nehemiah*, LIX). There are, however, some differences. For example, Ezra 6:18 states: "And they set the priests in their divisions and the Levites in their courses, for the service of God at Jerusalem, as it is written in the book of Moses." Although pentateuchal passages speak of the duties of priests and Levites (cf. Lev. 8; Num. 3:5-10), there is no *specific* mention of the structures mentioned in Ezra 6:18. According to 1 Chron. 23 – 26, this development is due to David. But, in general, it may be said that the law tradition in which Ezra was a "skilled" (perceptive) interpreter was the pentateuchal tradition. See further the discussion of C. Houtman, "Ezra and the Law," *OTS* 21 (1981) 91-115.

The Torah and Temple

In Ezra's emphasis on Law *(Torah)* we see the beginnings of a development that will find completion in the rabbinical literature of a much later time. It must be emphasized, however, that this "development" stands in strong continuity with the temple and its traditions. A life lived in accordance with the Law was an essential aspect of temple worship, as can be seen by the witness of many psalms (e.g., Pss. 1, 15, 19, 119). One might say that the temple was made for Law and not Law for the temple. Israel could survive without the temple, but she would cease to exist without the Law (Torah).

Torah Is Teaching

For some Christians, the Law *(Torah)* has a heavy, oppressive sound. This view of Torah is due in part to the use of the term "Law" as a translation of *Torah*. It is true, of course, that Torah is Law, but it is the *law of the covenant;* it is the Law for people who already are in relationship with God. Therefore, Torah is more than Law; it is teaching or instruction for a people whom God has delivered and called to be his own.

Paul's View of Torah

Paul's statements probably come first to our memory when we think of the Law (Torah) and postexilic Judaism; for example, see such words as the following:

"For the law brings wrath." (Rom. 4:15)

"Christ redeemed us from the curse of the law." (Gal. 3:13)

"Because by the works of the law shall no one be justified." (Gal. 2:16)

These words of Paul create a misunderstanding of the Jewish Law tradition because they are not interpreted in the context of Paul's purpose or audience. He speaks in opposition to some people who have a wrong view of the Law. They have forgotten the covenant setting of the Law and have turned it into a legality. The people that Paul attacks are likely those that Amos and Jeremiah would have opposed (see Rom. 2:17-29; cf. Jer. 7:1-28 and Amos 5:10-24).

Paul does make some affirmative statements about the Law (e.g., Rom. 3:31; 7:12), but because he is in conflict with those who misuse the Law, he chooses not to mention passages in the OT or in postbiblical Jewish literature that speak of the Law with warmth and love. For example, Paul nowhere refers to the following view of the Law:

The law of the LORD is perfect,
    reviving the soul;
the testimony of the LORD is sure,
    making wise the simple;
the precepts of the LORD are right,
    rejoicing the heart;
the commandment of the LORD is pure,
    enlightening the eyes;
the fear of the LORD is clean,
    enduring for ever;

57

the ordinances of the LORD are true,
  and righteous altogether.
More to be desired are they than gold,
  even much fine gold;
sweeter also than honey
  and drippings of the honeycomb. (Ps. 19:7-10; cf. Ps. 119)

The Law Creates Harmony

For the classical prophets, the psalmists, Ezra, and those following him, the Law was not a burden of legalistic requirements or
an expression of wrath. It was the gift of God to a people he had
rescued in the Exodus (Exod. 20:2). It was not a Law that killed,
but one that made alive; it was a way of ordering life so that a
community could live in harmony with God and each other. Life
in a community must have some structure; if it is not ordered in
one way (in terms of love and justice), it will be ordered in another manner.

Ezra 7:14, 25 point to the Law as a teaching that gives structure and good order to society. Ezra is sent by King Artaxerxes
"to make inquiries about Judah and Jerusalem according to the
law of your God, which is in your hand" (v. 14). We are not told
what prompted this mission. Quite likely some important community problems had come to the attention of Jewish leaders in
exile and Ezra requested that he be allowed to travel to Israel to
guide the community in its difficult time. The other possibility
is that the problems in the community made the king anxious
about the political stability of that area, so he sent Ezra there to
observe and correct the situation according to the teaching (i.e.,
the Law) in which Ezra was the expert.

The Law Is Divine Wisdom

In 7:25 this law is identified as "wisdom": "And you, Ezra, according to the wisdom of your God which is in your hand, appoint
magistrates and judges who may judge all the people." Ezra's
visit had political as well as religious overtones. But the basic
purpose of his trip was to establish a structure in the community
that conformed with God's "law" (v. 14) or "wisdom" (v. 25).
The Law as "wisdom" indicates that it is not a series of arbitrary
rules forced on people by a powerful God, but is rather a teaching
that is intended to establish order for the good of the community.
In succeeding centuries, Jews and Christians —living in new contexts — will reinterpret the Law for their times under the guidance

of God, but this does not invalidate the purpose or the "goodness" of the Law for the people living in the time of Ezra.

Law and Wisdom in Jewish and Christian Literature

In later Jewish literature, the close relationship between Law and wisdom, which we have seen in Ezra (7:14, 25), is reflected in a number of texts. According to Ecclesiasticus (sometimes called Sirach or Ben Sira), the wisdom of God settled down in Israel as Law (1:26-27; 24:8, 22; 33:2-3; cf. Bar. 4:1). This Torah-wisdom, according to some writers, was created before the world itself was brought into existence (Prov. 8:22-23; Sir. 24:3-4, 9; Wis. 7:25-26) and thus represents God's basic intention for the universe, that is, life rather than death. Jesus himself is closely related to Torah: in his life and teachings he fulfills the Torah (Matt. 5:17), and the NT writers refer to him in terms that are elsewhere applied to the Torah (e.g., John 6:35; 14:6). Further, Jesus is also identified as the "wisdom of God" (e.g., 1 Cor. 1:24; Luke 11:49). Although we should not read back all of these later interpretations into the text of Ezra, these subsequent developments continue basic thought patterns of the Jewish tradition and therefore give us insight into the character of law in Ezra.

Do the Law (7:10)

Ezra is a scribe who was "skilled in the law of Moses" (v. 6). He committed himself to study the Law (which is the divine wisdom) in order to *obey* its instructions. Further, he has given himself to teaching this Law to Israel so that Israel might *do* its wise teachings.

It is impossible to separate completely thought and deed, but one may say that Israelite-Jewish teaching is more concerned about doing, living, and acting than with correct concepts concerning God (i.e., right doctrine). The prophets reprove Israelites for not *doing* the law (e.g., Jer. 7:1-28; cf. also Rom. 2:17-24). Jesus makes the same emphasis in his teaching (cf. Luke 6:46-49; John 14:15; see also Rom. 2:17-24 and Jas. 1:22-25). Although authentic responses to God include the emotional and intellectual, without the deed these responses are judged to be inadequate by God. The God who acted and continues to act for his people can never be fully happy unless the acts of his own people create a community in which everyone may find liberation and fulfillment — salvation.

THE GENEROSITY OF ARTAXERXES (7:11-26)

Ezra: A Second Joseph

As Joseph, long ago, gained the trust of the pharaoh of Egypt and was enabled to preserve his family and clan, so Ezra won the friendship of the Persian king, Artaxerxes; it was a friendship that spelled survival for the postexilic Jewish community. Ezra, together with the group that he organized, was sent to Jerusalem at the command of the Persian king (vv. 13-14), who "granted him all that he asked" (7:6; cf. vv. 21-22).

The king himself offers gifts to the returning Jews so that they will be able to bring the proper sacrifices (vv. 14-20; contrast Exod. 10:25-27). In addition, Artaxerxes decrees that the temple staff shall be exempt from any kind of tax (v. 24). The king is in full support of anything that is to be done for the temple: "Whatever is commanded by the God of heaven, let it be done in full for the house of the God of heaven" (v. 23).

The King Expects Cooperation for His Support (7:23)

Persian generosity does not come from a heart overflowing with kindness, as we have said before. The king supports the work of the God of heaven among the former exiles "lest his wrath be against the realm of the king and his sons" (v. 23; cf. 6:10). From other documents we know that the Persians restored the gods of various peoples (i.e., their images) to their places and reestablished their sanctuaries in order to win the favor of these deities (see the Cyrus Cylinder, *ANET,* 315).

The Law of God and the King (7:25-26)

In addition to assisting the Jews in the continuance of temple worship by providing for sacrificial animals, Artaxerxes gives Ezra authority to establish judges who would uphold the law of God promulgated by Ezra. Although Ezra acts principally as a religious leader, he must have traveled to Israel as some kind of official of the Persian ruler. This would explain the action of Artaxerxes that places the power of the Persian empire behind the reform project of Ezra. The king decrees that severe punishment will be carried out (including execution) on those who "will not obey the law of your God and the law of the king" (7:26). Breaking the law — whether Persian law or the law of God — earned the same punishment.

Although some passages in the OT speak of a close relationship between the commands of an Israelite king and those of God (e.g., Prov. 24:21), a new element has entered the Jewish community through the decree of Artaxerxes, namely, a foreign ruler who does not worship Yahweh nevertheless establishes a policy that demands obedience to Yahweh on pain of punishment. Religious and political disobedience is punished by the authority of the Persian government and with the same kinds of punishment.

State Policy and the "I-Thou" Relationship

Jewish cooperation with Persian rule has its dangers. It is especially dangerous when the state punishes people for disobedience to religious principles. This *state policy* of Persia threatened the covenantal, "I-Thou" relationship. The danger was very much present in early and later Christianity. The legalization of Christianity under Constantine and the support of the Christian faith by governments in other lands (e.g., in Germany) have obscured and undercut the character of Christianity. Such is the danger today regarding any contemporary state policy that would exact fines or punishment on people who violate some Christian teaching. *Ironically, by requiring everyone to obey God, the relationship between God and people is destroyed.* State-sponsored religion attacks the core of faith. Martin Buber's comments on the Ten Commandments apply to religious teaching generally: "The Ten Commandments are not part of an impersonal codex governing an association of men. They were uttered by an *I* and addressed to a *Thou.* . . . *Nothing of its [i.e., society's] vast machinery has anything to do with the situation of the human being who in the midst of a personal experience hears and feels himself addressed by the word 'thou' "* (*On the Bible*, 18).

Ezra's Policy: Cooperation or Collaboration?

Although Ezra and those who favored his program of reform may have welcomed the support of the Persian government, some other Jews must have viewed this close working relationship with the Persians as a collaborationist program (see Paul Hanson, *Dawn of Apocalyptic*, 226, 273-76). Ezra's decision to endure this interference of the Persian state, while understandable, strikes a bit of irony. In connection with some Jews and all foreigners in the land, he pursues a policy of separation, but with the Persians he demonstrates generous appreciation (Ezra 6:14), cooperation, and subservience (7:26), which manifests itself even in the cult where prayer was offered for the king and his sons (see 6:10; the king requested this prayer and most likely it was offered). If admission of non-exiled Jews or foreigners into the community represented a threat to pure religion, this cooperation with Persia was not without risk.

The early Israelite laws that call for separation from foreigners in the land (e.g., Exod. 23:23-33 and Deut. 7:1-3; cf. Ezra 9:12) hardly give direct encouragement to the pro-Persian policy of Ezra. Although it might be said that this policy had some roots in the prophetic tradition that spoke of Yahweh chosing certain foreign leaders to accomplish his purpose (e.g., Nebuchadnezzar and Cyrus; cf. Jer. 27:6 and Isa. 45:1), one would hardly think that the prophets who made these announcements had in mind a continuing, cooperative policy of the type recorded in the book of Ezra.

Commonsense Theology

The tenuous existence of the Jewish community in the postexilic period must have made Jewish leaders open to options that they otherwise would not have considered. If Israel had been stronger and more certain of her future, is it likely that she would have included prayers for Persian royalty, allowed the Persian state to punish violators of Jewish law, or even have been so uncritical of the Persian regime? I do not think so. But, in times of need, people frequently extend themselves to take actions that they would never have considered in another siutation. Elias Bickermann provides insight into actions of Jews of this period (and perhaps into the actions of people generally): "In fact, being real men and not puppets like the characters portrayed in conventional textbooks, the Jews of the Restoration, like those of every generation, were entangled in contradictions and in conflicting patterns of real life" (*From Ezra to the Last of the Maccabees*, 16).

At the Right Time

Joseph was in Egypt at the right time to save his family — and all of future Israel — from extinction. The Israelites (of the time of Joshua) entered the land of Palestine just at the right time to establish a foothold there; no great power was on the scene to stop them. David arose to kingship at the right time because there was a power vacuum in Syria-Palestine at that time. Christianity was born at the right religious and political time to establish itself as a worldwide religion. The rise of the Persians in the ancient world represented a right time for the Jews as well as for other captive peoples in the ancient Near East. Their benevolent rule (even if faulted by self-interest) enabled the Jews to return to the land, rebuild the temple, and set up a community based on traditions rooted in the ancient soil of Israelite faith. Bickerman observes: "The imperial protection [i.e., of the Persians] shielded Palestinian Jewry from the Arabs and the Philistines, Edom and Moab. . . . If Jerusalem had not been a part of a Gentile empire, the nomads would have driven the Jews into the sea or swallowed up Palestine" (*From Ezra to the Last of the Maccabees,* 10).

But There Are Wrong Times

One must take care about developing a theology of a "right time" happening to people who serve God because, as we look over history, we see many "wrong times" for individuals and groups. Blacks, Jews, the aged, Indians, Armenians, women, minority groups everywhere, as well as the majority of people in the world — the poor — offer more than enough illustrations of such periods. A simplistic theology of the "right time" for God's people would be an additional cruel blow to those who have had more than enough pain. But even people who suffer many "wrong times" know some "salvation" times when something right is happening. The biblical authors celebrate the "right times" as gifts from God even though they know that the other times occur.

Right Times Are Times for Action

Now and then, "right times" are surprises that bring blessing to us through no effort of our own, but often they are of little profit unless people recognize them and *risk action.* The rise of the Persians was a right time for the Jews, but without devout people willing to risk themselves in building a new temple and settling the land, this time would have passed by without consequence. The Jews saw this period of history as an occasion — an opportunity — for a future, and they worked in cooperation with God to achieve that future.

Other Jews during this period responded differently to what was happening. Paul Hanson speaks about the "visionaries" of the exilic period who, opposing the program proposed by Ezekiel and those following him, "delineated the restoration in very vague terms, attributing all to Yahweh's glorious acts rather than spelling out particular historical details" (*Dawn of Apocalyptic,* 176). They were waiting for God himself to act — and in his own fashion to establish his way in the world. This is not to say that they ruled out the participation of people in "God's program"; but how people were to work with God was left indistinct. Because this was so, any *specific program* presented was perceived as falling short of what God would do when he acted. A similar situation obtains in the present day. Some pious Jews oppose the state of Israel, because, as they view it, the restoration of Israel should come about by an act of God instead of through the efforts of people.

God Alone or God with People?

Every age experiences the conflict between those who say, "God needs us to build up Zion," and those who testify, "God will act soon to establish his kingdom; we leave everything to God." The "God alone people" criticize the former for assuming too great an importance in what is really God's program — for identifying too simply their work with God's work.

These futurists, who leave everything to God, are criticized in turn for being of no "earthly" good. Age after age these people long for a "special intervention" of God that will cut through the ambiguities and wrongs of human society to establish his will alone — but this hope sometimes blinds them to what should and must be done now. In the face of cruelty and injustice, often the best these people can do is to hope that "somehow" God will take action. The classical prophets and Ezra-Nehemiah clearly regard God as the one who *does* work his will in the world, but they also recognize that he looks to human beings as his partners in establishing *shalom* in this world.

A NEW EXODUS
Ezra 8:1-36

EZRA AND THE TWELVE LEAVE BABYLON (8:1-14)

Ezra's personal reminiscences about his mission begin in 7:27-28, where he praises God, who inspired the Persian king to act on behalf of the exiles. Confident that "the hand of the LORD" was with him, he called upon the Jewish leaders to "go up" with him to Israel. These leaders are mentioned in 8:1 as the "heads of their fathers' houses." The listing of twelve families may be a conscious effort on the part of Ezra to connect this return to the land with the traditions concerning the twelve tribes under Moses.

A Son of David Returns with Ezra (8:2)

Hattush, a descendant of David (cf. 1 Chron. 3:22), is mentioned as a member of the returning exiles, but he is *only mentioned!* There is no additional comment concerning him, here or elsewhere. Hattush is not singled out for special attention; although he is descended from David, he is not considered to be a possible future ruler. The writings of Ezra and Nehemiah lack any explicit hope for a ruler from the house of David. Memory of the failure of Zerubbabel (see our discussion in ch. 5) quieted such expectations and changed the priorities of the community. The most important people are the priests. One indication of their place of honor is that they are listed first among the families returning to the land (i.e., the families of Phinehas and Ithamar, 8:2). Standing in the second rank is the family of David represented by Hattush. Davidic descendants are accorded a place of honor, but not of the kind given to Zerubbabel in the books of Haggai and Zechariah.

Jewish Literature: Diverse Hopes for the Future

The books of Ezra and Nehemiah are reminders that within the Hebrew scriptures are varied expectations for the present and future. The figure of David looms large in some literature of the OT (cf., e.g ., Isa. 9:2-7; 11:1-3), but in Ezekiel, Ezra, and Nehemiah, the priests are in charge.

One sees even greater diversity of future expectations in later Jewish literature which speaks of: a priest (T. Levi 18); a priest and a royal figure, with the priest as superior to the royal representative (T. Judah 21, 24; cf. Ezek. 44 – 46); three eschatological figures: prophet, Davidic ruler, and priest (4QTestim); the Son of Man (1 Enoch 37 – 71); and Melchizedek (11QMelch). These varied expressions of hope appear also in the NT. Jesus is depicted as: the Davidic Messiah (e.g., Matt. 21:5, 9); the Son of Man (e.g., Mark 14:61-62); the Priest (e.g., Heb. 4:14); the Prophet (e.g., Acts 3:17-23; see also Matt. 16:13-14); and Melchizedek (Heb. 6:19-20).

Although in Christian circles the Davidic Messiah became the dominant expression of future expectation, in late pre-Christian Judaism and in the Judaism of the Common Era, hope for the future exhibited great variety. The brief outline in the above paragraph is informed by the excellent discussion of George Nickelsburg and Michael Stone in *Faith and Piety in Early Judaism: Texts and Documents*, 161-202.

THE JOURNEY HOME (8:15-36)

Levites Are Missing (8:15-20)

In preparation for the journey to Israel, Ezra gathers the people by a river in the region. Looking over those accompanying him, he notices that no Levites are present. He then makes special effort to enlist this clergy as participants in the return to the homeland. He sends influential people ("leading men" and "men of insight," v. 16) with special instructions to speak to Iddo and his kin about recruiting Levites (vv. 16-17). Iddo was "the leading man at the place Casiphia" (v. 17). This community pressure resulted in thirty-eight Levites joining Ezra's group. Earlier seventy-four Levites had returned under Zerubbabel (Ezra 2:40), and a later time reveals that two hundred and eighty-four Levites were in the land. The last number, however, included temple singers (Neh. 10:10-11), so we have no exact figure on the Levites as a separate group. With the Zadokite priests numbering 4,289 in the Jewish community, it is apparent that the Levites are not well represented.

The Absence of Levites: Explanations

Why did so few Levites elect to return to the land? Two observations deserve attention: (1) There may not have been many Levites living in exile. After the devastation of Judah, the Babylonians sent into exile Judah's leaders (i.e., royalty, priests, and the upper classes), leaving the country in the hands of the poor and powerless (2 Kgs. 24:14). This group probably included the Levites. With the priests deported, the Levites became the clergy to whom people looked for guidance. They played a leading role in any worship that took place, possibly serving as "priests" at the ruined altar where people still worshiped (cf. Jer. 41:4-5; see Roland de Vaux, *Ancient Israel: Its Life and Institutions*, 387). Paul Hanson suggests that Isa. 63:18 refers to this situation when the Levites ("your holy people") held control of the altar in the land of Israel (*Dawn of Apocalyptic*, 96, 227). (2) Levites were in conflict with the Zadokite priests who dominated the postexilic community. This dissension may be seen in Ezek. 44, where the Levitical clergy are denigrated (44:9-14) and the Zadokite priests are exalted (vv. 15-16).

Opposition Parties: Levites and Zadokites

The struggle between these two groups probably dates back to the preexilic period. In fact, according to Roland de Vaux, Jer. 7 reflects the estrangement between the Zadokites and the Levites (*Ancient Israel*, 376). Jeremiah comes from the Levitical city of Anathoth (Josh. 21:18) and addresses threatening words to the Zadokite priests who have placed their trust in the temple rather than in Yahweh. It is the attack of one who is sympathetic to the Levitical tradition. An early postexilic oracle continues Jeremiah's sharp criticism of those who exalt the temple above the God of the covenant (Isa. 66:5-6). Although we cannot be certain, the latter passage may be a judgment on the Zadokites that rises out of the Levitical or "visionary" community, as suggested by Paul Hanson (*Dawn of Apocalyptic*, 223-28, 254, 261).

Some Levites Returned. Why?

In the light of the negative view of the Levites in Ezek. 44:9-14, it is no surprise that so few of them returned to the land to serve in the temple. But some did return. Why? Did they come back because they could see change taking place? Did they see themselves as persons chosen to bring about this change? We do not know. It is apparent, however, that by the time of Ezra and Nehemiah the Zadokites and some of the Levites are reconciled. The books of Ezra, Nehemiah, and Chronicles portray the Levites very positively. Although the community is under the leadership of the Zadokite priests, there is no denigration of the Levites. They are depicted as faithful, Torah-true servants of Yahweh (cf. Neh. 8:9, 13; 2 Chron. 29:34) — a reputation that goes back to the time of Moses when the Levites stood with Moses and Yahweh over against the idolatrous actions of Aaron the priest (Exod. 32:26).

Faith Turns to Fear (8:21-23)

With the addition of the Levites and the temple servants, Ezra is ready to begin the journey to Israel. But, as he is about to depart, the dangers of the trip cause him anxiety. Earlier, in a burst of enthusiasm, he had spoken to the Persian king about this trip and had expressed confidence that God would take care of them: "The hand of our God is for good upon all that seek him, and the power of his wrath is against all that forsake him" (v. 22). Now, however, on the verge of leaving, fear strikes him, but he is "ashamed" to request help from the king because he had seemed so certain of God's protection. To ask for an accompanying band of soldiers would appear to be a denial of his confidence in God. He decides, therefore, not to ask for a troop of soldiers to guard them.

Ezra, the strong, decisive reformer, comes close to us in this very human moment. Here, as elsewhere in the biblical witness, we see a mixture of strength and weakness. Confidence and optimism may easily be succeeded by self-doubt and great anxiety (see, e.g., the fearfulness of Elijah following his courageous confrontation with the prophets of Baal on Mt. Carmel, 2 Kgs. 19:1-3).

Fasting and Prayer in Time of Danger

Ezra calls a fast, an act that is frequently resorted to in times of oppression (Ps. 69:10; 109:24), fateful decision (Matt. 4:2; Acts 13:2-3), or threat, as here (cf. Joel 1:14; 2 Chron. 20:3). Herbert Ryle describes the significance of this practice: "Ezra appoints the fast (a) as the symbol of submission before God's will and of repentance from sin, (b) as the means of intensifying religious fervour in prayer through the restraint laid upon the physical appetite, (c) as the testimony that 'man lives not by bread alone' " (*Ezra and Nehemiah*, 106).

The Past Is Happening Again

The caravan leaves the camp, and, after a long and dangerous journey, they arrive safely in the land. Earlier, Second Isaiah had declared that the Yahweh of the Exodus would rise again in power to protect the exiles who would return to the land (Isa. 40:9-11; 41:8-16). His words proved true for Ezra and for those who accompanied him; the divine "hand" that guided the early Israelites out of Egypt (cf. Deut. 5:15) had lost none of its power (Ezra 8:22, 31)!

A New Exodus?

In Isa. 40 – 55, without doubt, the prophet thinks of the return from the Exile as a second Exodus from a second Egypt, that is, Babylon (see, e.g., 42:13-16; 43:14-21; 52:1-2, 11-12). Although one can speak of a sustained "exodus theme" in this prophecy, it is questionable whether one can do the same for the books of Ezra and Nehemiah. Nevertheless, the latter writings exhibit an awareness that what is happening in the postexilic period is related to Israel's early life. There is memory of early laws (Ezra 9:12; cf. Deut. 7:3), the building of the tabernacle (Ezra 2:68-69; cf. Exod. 35:4-29), the twelve tribes (Ezra 2:2 par. Neh. 7:7; cf. Num. 1:20-43), Moses and the Torah (Neh. 8:1-2; cf. Exod. 24:3).

The Exodus is remembered also. In addition to the explicit references in Neh. 9:9, 17, 18, there may be allusions to this event elsewhere, for example: (1) Like the Hebrews in Egypt, the exiles knew what it was to be slaves (Ezra 9:9; cf. Deut. 6:21 and 26:6-8). (2) The departure from Babylonian slavery took place in the first month of the year, as did the Exodus from Egypt (Ezra 7:9; cf. Exod. 12:2). (3) In the present text (8:31) there is memory of a time long ago when Yahweh surrounded the Hebrews with his protection (Exod. 13:21; cf. Isa. 52:12) and delivered them from those who would destroy them.

Klaus Koch declares that "Ezra's march from Babylonia to Jerusalem was a cultic procession which Ezra understood as a second Exodus and a partial fulfillment of prophetic expectations" ("Ezra and the Origins of Judaism," *JSS* 29 [1974]: 184). In view of Ezra 8:24-30, which emphasizes the holy character of the priests and the vessels they are to carry (cf. Isa. 52:11-12), this suggestion deserves consideration. But the evidence is sparse and we fall short of certainty at this point. It is inconceivable, however, that those returning to the land from Babylon would have overlooked the "similarities" that existed between the events of their day and those of the time of Moses.

Hope for the future is often based on the events of the past. This is a main theme in Israel's thought, as is demonstrated by the Psalms and the oracles of the prophets. The God of the Then is the God of the Now. Out of this confidence the former exiles lived; it is this conviction that carries along people of faith today.

INTERMARRIAGE
Ezra 9:1-15

THE REFUSAL TO SEPARATE FROM
THE NATIONS (9:1-2)

Some time after Ezra's arrival in the land ("After these things," v. 1), he was confronted by the problem of assimilation. The "leaders" *(sarim)* of the community, who perhaps were working with Ezra, reported to him concerning the negligence of some priests, Levites, and laypersons. These people were lax in keeping themselves separate from foreigners (i.e., "the peoples of the lands") and from their traditions, which are labeled "their abominations." We are not told what these abominations are, but an indication of their character may be derived from the following passage, which speaks of the "abominations of those nations" (Deut. 18:9-14; cf. 1 Kgs. 14:21-24). The lifestyle of these people opposes that of the Torah community of Israel as death opposes life (Deut. 30:15-20; Ps. 1).

The "Canaanites" Are Alive Again!

The listing of these nations in v. 1 (i.e., "Canaanites . . . Amorites") is influenced by earlier lists of Israel's enemies (see, e.g., Deut. 7:1-5, which includes five of the nations mentioned here). The Deuteronomic narrative commands that strict separation be maintained between these people and the Israelites; in fact, it stipulates that the non-Israelites are to be killed. By the time of Ezra, however, these five nations no longer existed as identifiable groups. In addition to the names of these ancient peoples, the Ezra text includes Ammonites, Moabites, and Egyptians. They too are considered to be old enemies of Israel (Deut. 23:3-7). Unlike the other five nations listed, however, these groups still existed in the 5th century B.C.E. and may have been represented among "the peoples of the lands." In any case "the peoples of the lands" are identified with Israel's ancient enemies. The "Canaanites . . . Amorites" are alive again! They threatened the existence of Israel in the early days, and now, at the time of Israel's new beginning, they menace the people of God once more. These opponents never die, nor do they fade away; they are always present in one form or another. People of faith must make decisions concerning these people and their way of life (see, e.g., Ps. 1 and Deut. 30:15-20).

Danger: Intermarriage

The refusal of some laypersons, priests, and Levites to "separate" from the foreigners resulted in a dangerous situation for the community, whose possibility of survival was already tenuous: *intermarriage*. Although the foreign marriages of some of Israel's leaders (e.g., Joseph and David) are not denounced in the Bible, these alliances were not considered normal practice in Israel. It was, however, a constant temptation for Israel. Even Moses, the great lawgiver, took a woman from Cush as his wife. Miriam and Aaron, who probably represented a larger group within the community, critized Moses for this act (Num. 12:1). We do not, however, learn anything more about this situation because the text moves to a different focus. Marriages with foreign women did take place from time to time, but such unions carried obvious dangers to the community. More so than today in the Western world, marriage was a family affair; the man "joined" the family of his wife and the wife the family of her husband. The Jewish husband who becomes a part of his foreign wife's family will certainly be influenced by his father-in-law and brothers- and sisters-in-law (Ezra 9:12; cf. Deut. 7:4).

The Laxity of Leaders

No doubt, the number of people involved in intermarriage was not large, but it may have been larger than the 113 persons (out of approximately 50,000 returnees) listed in Ezra 10. Those listed may only represent the people who cooperated with Ezra. Nevertheless, even if the number was small, these marriages threatened the special character of the Jewish community because those entering such marriages were priests, Levites, and, probably, upper-class laypersons ("people," 9:1; see H. L. Ellison, *From Babylon to Bethlehem*, 49). The leaders of Jewish society would have the most contact with foreign peoples, be under the greatest temptation to develop close relationships, and be influential enough (so they believed) to enter into a mixed marriage without fear of criticism. Perhaps Ezra would not have become so disturbed by mixed marriages if they had not involved the elite of the community (v. 2). But when the leaders of the community lead in the wrong direction — one that involves the rejection of Torah — then Ezra, following the example of the prophets (see, e.g., Hos. 4:4-5; 5:1-2), was compelled to oppose their actions. A covenant community that allows its leaders to adopt a lifestyle that threatens the central covenant-Torah traditions is sacrificing its future.

Who Is a Jew?

Verse 2 declares that the "holy race [or "holy seed" — *zera` haqqodesh*] has mixed itself with the peoples of the lands"; Jewish men were marrying foreign women. Daniel J. Silver (*A History of Judaism,* 1:161) observes that the actions of Ezra "had something to do with 'blood.' " The importance given to genealogical information in Ezra 2:1-63 and 8:1-14 points in this direction as does the use of the word "seed." Those who belong to the Jewish community are Jews — persons who come from Jewish bloodlines. Even if one allows for the admittance of proselytes (who therefore are not of Jewish blood), they are the exceptions that prove the rule.

The marriage of a Jewish man to a foreign woman caused great anxiety in Ezra because of the close relationship the children in such a marriage would have to the non-Jewish mother. Because she was foreign she would not teach her children Hebrew (cf. Neh.. 13:23-24) or reflect the life and thought of the Jewish tradition. Only a Jewish mother would and could do that. Later on, Jewish tradition would decree that a Jew is one who is born of a Jewish mother (see B.T. *Yebamoth* 23a; cf. Acts 16:1-3 regarding Timothy). The fact that the child "came from" the Jewish mother in a very physical sense must have played a role in establishing that definition. But another factor probably played an important part in setting up this tradition: the Jewish community knew that children who "grew up" Jewish usually had Jewish mothers. The fear of mixed marriage reflected concern not only for the individuals who took part in this union; it had to do also with the future of the Jewish family and community. Marriage to a non-Jewish woman, it was believed, placed in question the Jewishness of the children born to that marriage and threatened family loyalty to Jewish traditions.

Is Ezra out of Step with the Wider Israelite Tradition?

Ezra's focus on intermarriage often appears to the modern reader as a wrong emphasis — an underscoring of what is peripheral. It is, we think, the view of a narrow-minded community — a community turned in on itself. But it is likely that the major prophets of Israel (e.g., Isaiah, Jeremiah, and Amos) would have also opposed intermarriage in the situation that Ezra faced. We do not, however, have any direct information on this subject in these prophetic writings. The only explicit prophetic word directed against intermarriage is found in the postexilic writing of Malachi (2:10-16).

The confession of Ezra, however, may throw some light on the subject. He declares: "For we have forsaken thy commandments, which thou didst command *by thy servants the prophets*" (vv. 10b-11a). Even though the text that follows this confession (vv. 11b-12) is formed mostly on the basis of Torah material, Ezra's reference to *"thy servants the prophets"* suggests that his opposition to intermarriage is that of the prophets as well. Certainly the prophets were at one with Ezra in condemning those in Israel who adopted the "ways" of the nations (see, e.g., Ezek. 23:30; Jer. 10:1-3). With such negative views of the non-Jewish nations, they would hardly approve of Jews marrying foreigners.

At times, interpreters set the universalism of the book of Jonah over against the writings of Ezra and Nehemiah. But it would be an error to think that the author of the book of Jonah had no concerns about the dangers of intermarriage. Although this brief prophetic book may be a critique of an ingrown Jewish community, it is unlikely that the author embraced a universalism that would have counted the *Jewish* family tradition as unimportant.

Assimilation Today: Judaism

In the present day, the three major divisions of Judaism (Orthodox, Conservative, and Reform) are seriously concerned about intermarriage. Dow Marmur speaks for the whole community when he says: "Therefore, the greatest danger to Jewish survival outside Israel today is not anti-Semitism but assimilation, epitomized by the threat of intermarriage . . . [it] is a direct threat to Judaism, *for without Jews Judaism cannot exist*" (*Intermarriage*, 2; emphasis mine).

Intermarriage: The Church

Mixed marriages and the children that result from them are not to be isolated as Jewish problems. It is an important issue for the Christian Church as well. We have no word from Jesus on this subject, but it is hard to believe that he would have approved of

74

intermarriage. The early church was forced to confront it. Paul calls upon believers to separate themselves from those outside the Christian community:

> Do not be mismated with unbelievers. For what partnership have righteousness and iniquity? Or what fellowship has light with darkness? What accord has Christ with Belial? Or what has a believer in common with an unbeliever? (2 Cor. 6:14-15; see also vv. 16-18)

The repetitive questions underscore the firmness of the apostle on this issue. Like Ezra, Paul knew the dangers of intermarriage; he feared a weakening of the community of faith in the present (by means of the influence of the "unbeliever" on the "believer") and loss in the future because the children who grow up in these homes are influenced by a mixed tradition. But his urging falls on some deaf ears; believers marry unbelievers and have children. Paul addresses this difficult problem and gives teaching for a situation that he hoped could have been avoided (1 Cor. 7:12-16). He does the best he can in a complicated situation—he has no word from the Lord (a remembered saying of Jesus?). Paul affirms that the believer in the marriage makes the unbelieving spouse holy and therefore the children resulting from the marriage are holy. The exact meaning of this passage is difficult to assess, but in it we can see Paul's concern for the children of such a marriage. He does not wish to see these children lost to Christ and the Church.

Intermarriage: A Threat to Lifegiving Traditions

Intermarriage, then, is not just the affair of the two people who marry. It has importance for the whole community, present and future, especially when very different traditions are involved (as was the case, e.g., of the Jews in the time of Ezra and of Christians in the 1st century).

Minority communities, such as those mentioned above, probably see more clearly the effects of intermarriage than do the majority communities (e.g., the Christian church in the United States). But intermarriage has an effect on every community, and the words of Ezra, Nehemiah, and Paul have import for the community of faith today. Although such a marriage may have a beneficial effect on the community, frequently it presents a danger because one partner of this "one body" cannot affirm (or perhaps actively opposes) the traditions that enliven the community.

EZRA'S RESPONSE TO THE PEOPLE'S
UNFAITHFULNESS (9:3-15)

Ezra's response to this unfaithfulness, depicted in vv. 3-4, is that of one struck by disaster. As a person staggered by grief at the death of a family member (Job 1:20; cf. Gen. 37:34) or shocked upon hearing ruinous news (Esth. 4:1), Ezra tears at his clothes and pulls out his hair (v. 3). These are frenzied acts that one may observe today in those who have been shattered by death or betrayal. Ezra sits "appalled," as one struck by terror, "until the evening sacrifice" (v. 4; cf. v. 3 and Ezek. 3:15). With this reference to "sacrifice" we become aware that Ezra's violence to himself is not merely a personal response. His acts have cultic significance; they are symbolic actions that express, more than words could ever do, Yahweh's anger and pain at viewing this apostasy.

As he sits in stunned silence, he is joined by those who have remained loyal (v. 4: "all who trembled at the words of the God of Israel"). With this "congregation" he observes the "evening sacrifice," and then he rose from his "fasting" (NEB "humiliation"). The Hebrew word translated "fasting" *(ta'anith)* is found only here in the OT. Although in postbiblical Jewish literature it occurs very often with the meaning of "fasting," in the present text (while abstinence from food is to be assumed) the emphasis is upon Ezra's grieving self-abasement, which is signified by the special character of his sitting (silent and motionless?). The cultic character of Ezra's behavior is underscored by his further actions; while still wearing his torn clothes, he falls to his knees and spreads out his hands (v. 5) and prays to God in the holy space that surrounds the temple (cf. 10:1).

Opposition That Really Hurts

It is never enjoyable to have others stand against us, but when opposition comes from people that we have trusted and depended on, then the pain is sharp and deep. Ezra knows the feeling. The people who have cast aside the teaching that calls for separation from the nations are the "returned exiles" (v. 4); their leaders are the leading offenders (v. 2). The people rescued from exile and brought back to the holy land are once again succumbing to the seductions of the nations, failing to heed the warning of the Torah. Deuteronomy 7:4 speaks of Yahweh's threatened destruction to the nation if she did not maintain separation from the nations; that judgment finally came, according to the biblical authors, when Judah fell in 587 B.C.E.

Old Faithlessness Threatens the Future (9:6-15)

Now, just when the Jews are on the eve of a new day, the old faithlessness reasserts itself and places a question mark over the future. The people of God — some of them, at least — have not learned from the past. They should know and act better, but they do not. Ezra, representing the whole community, is "ashamed" (v. 6) to call upon God because he has been more than kind to them. Although he punished the people because of their long, continued sinfulness (v. 7), he has in recent days acted with compassion and has brought the exiles back to the land. During this "brief moment" in the land, the exiles (the "remnant," vv. 8, 13, 15) have been able to rebuild the temple and to establish a secure community in Judah and Jerusalem (vv. 8-9).

But now, after a brief time in the land, the Jews go back to their old rebellious ways. They forsake the teaching of God concerning separation from the nations even to the extent of entering into marriages with foreign people (vv. 10-12; cf. vv. 1-2 and Deut. 7:1-3). Following God's grace-beyond-grace action in restoring the people to the land ("punishing us less than our iniquities deserved," v. 13), this kind of behavior is especially shocking. The profound shame that Ezra feels is reflected in the hyperbolic confession to God: "our iniquities have risen higher than our heads, and our guilt has mounted up to the heavens" (v. 6). To identify these words as hyperbole (exaggerated speech) is not, however, to indicate that they are to be taken lightly. The opposite is true. It is when normal speech fails us in describing some action or situation that we move to hyperbole. In this case, it reflects a depth of pain that routine words and imagery could never carry. Caution is needed, however; we should not interpret Ezra's words in a literalistic manner. See our "Special Note" at the end of this chapter.

Does Divine Patience Ever Come to An End? (9:14)

Ezra believes that if the apostasy is allowed to continue, it would threaten the existence of the community. He prays: "Wouldst thou not be angry with us till thou wouldst consume us, so that there should be no remnant, nor any to escape?" The implied answer is: "Yes." Ezra's drastic action in confronting mixed marriages in ch. 10 must be understood in the light of this belief that the final end would come unless the community reaffirmed the ancient teaching on separation from the nations.

The "Just" God and Savior (9:15)

When people have true sorrow for their faithless ways, God responds with forgiveness. This is part of what it means for him to be "just" (Heb. *tsaddiq*). Because God's justice is, at center, mercy, people who have sinned can call on God to forgive them *because* of his just character (cf. Dan. 9:15-16). In the latter text the RSV translation "righteous acts" renders the Heb. *tsidqotheka*. Further, when people have experienced forgiveness and deliverance, they rejoice in his righteousness (cf. Ps. 51:14). The RSV translation "thy deliverance" reflects the Hebrew word *tsidqotheka*.

Ezra does not cover up Israel's rebellious behavior as he rehearses Israel's relationship with God. She has sinned and she deserves severe punishment, but, amazingly, God does not give her what she deserves. Even in judgment, his mercy is present. But what we call "mercy" Ezra designates as the "just" character of God. Ezra declares: "O LORD the God of Israel, thou art just *[tsaddiq]*, for we are left a remnant that has escaped, as at this day." If God had not been "just" there would not have been a remnant. But Ezra knows that he and his people are guilty in God's sight. They cannot, nor can anyone else, *stand* before God, that is, as if one had a right to God's favor. Psalm 130 is a commentary on the last half of v. 15: "If thou, O LORD, shouldst mark iniquities, Lord, who could stand? But there is forgiveness with thee, that thou mayest be feared" (vv. 3-4). If God had marked the iniquities of Israel (or the Church!) all hope would have been lost. But God's justice does not operate in that manner; it works — as long as possible — through forgiveness.

SPECIAL NOTE ON 9:13

In the midst of a long prayer to God, Ezra confesses: "thou, our God, hast punished us less than our iniquities deserved." We should take care not to literalize this confession. We are not intended to conclude that Israel was especially sinful and that in addition to the destruction of the state, the killing of many Israelites, and the exile of the leading citizens who survived, there should have been further punishment. Observe, by the way, that Second Isaiah takes a different view of Israel and her sins. When he speaks to Israelites suffering through exile in Babylon, he declares that Jerusalem "has received from the LORD's hand *double* for all her sins" (Isa. 40:2). Both Ezra 9:13 and Isa. 40:2 are examples of hyperbole — exaggerated speech.

The confession in Ezra 9:13 comes from a devout person who has a heartfelt sorrow for past sins. Ezra does not spare himself or his people; he does not try to justify himself or the Jewish community. He reflects the spirit of the Prodigal Son who confesses to his father (Luke 15:21), "I have sinned against heaven and before you; *I am no longer worthy* to be called your son." Devout people often exaggerate the extent of their wickedness (sometimes it is done to such an extent that it becomes an illness!) even though what they have done is no more serious than what others have done. The Prodigal Son (in Jesus' parable) looks at himself and *sees* how great the evil is and makes his confession. We might think him very bad, but he ranks above the Elder Brother who is unwilling to recognize and confess *his* sins.

Similarly, in another of Jesus' stories (Luke 18:9-14), the Tax Collector — by his own admission! — is very evil, but not nearly so bad as some Pharisees who will not bow the knee and heart before God. The sins of Israel, the sins of the Jewish community, are the sins of all people in every age. When we look at the wickedness which is present not only in Christian civilization but within the Church itself, we know that the Jewish community was in no sense unique in its ability to initiate shocking sinful acts. The confessions of sin in Ezra, and in the Hebrew Bible as a whole, reveal a remarkable ability to be self-critical; they illustrate what Jesus emphasized so strongly in the above two stories, that is, people who confess their sins and change their ways are the people who are pleasing to God. These confessions are models for both the Synagogue and the Church.

PRAYER, FIRM ACTION, AND REPENTANCE

Ezra 10:1-44

A PRAYER TO GOD IS "HEARD" BY THE JEWS (10:1)

Ezra's prayer in 9:6-15 is a prayer of confession (vv. 6-7) and thanksgiving (vv. 8-9) addressed to God, but it is also "preaching" intended for the ears of those about him (esp. vv. 10-15). The prayer is offered "before the house of God" because the temple, more than any other place, symbolizes the presence of Yahweh. Biblical writers use careful language when they speak about Yahweh's relationship to the temple. The temple does not restrict — it cannot hold — the fullness of his presence (1 Kgs. 8:27); nevertheless, it is his special place on earth. His "glory" and his "name" are there (1 Kgs. 8:11, 29; see Samuel Terrien, *The Elusive Presence*, 161-226). God hears those prayers that are offered while facing the temple, yes, he hears "in heaven" which is his "dwelling place" (1 Kgs. 8:29-30; cf. 2 Chron. 20:9).

As he prays, Ezra weeps and prostrates himself. It is the prayer of "a broken and contrite heart" (Ps. 51:17) — a prayer addressed to God (who prizes such a heart) and "heard" by "a very great assembly" of people who "wept bitterly."

IN REAL REPENTANCE LIES HOPE (10:2-5)

A representative of this group, Shecaniah, confesses the faithlessness of the community that is reflected in the marriage of Jewish men with "foreign women" (v. 2). Despite the seriousness of the sin, however, Shecaniah is convinced that the community can avoid judgment if the people pledge to God (i.e., "make a covenant" with God) that they will "put away" (lit. "bring out"; cf. v. 19 and Deut. 24:1-2) the foreign wives and their children. On behalf of the community, Shecaniah calls upon Ezra to take the lead in initiating this new action (v. 4). Ezra gathers "the

80

chiefs of the priests, the Levites, and all the Israelites" (NEB) and swears them to the support of this program (v. 5).

REAL REPENTANCE CREATES CHANGE (10:6-17)

Following Ezra's night of fasting in "the chamber of Jehohanan" (probably a priest who had a room in the temple complex), it is announced that "all the returned exiles" are to gather at Jerusalem "within three days." Those who did not respond would have their property confiscated and they themselves would be "banned from the congregation of the exiles" (vv. 6-8). "All the men" obey the proclamation and assemble "in the open square before the house of God" in Jerusalem. Ezra calls upon them to confess their sin and to separate themselves from the foreigners — especially from their "foreign wives" (vv. 9-11). The people agree to Ezra's demand (and that of the other leaders; cf. vv. 2-4), but they request additional time for consideration because of the "rain" (see the discussion in the following paragraph) and because "so grave an offence" (NEB) cannot be handled in a few days. They suggest that a commission made up of leaders from local communities and from the larger community meet with those who have married foreign women (vv. 12-14). Although this recommendation is not unanimously affirmed (v. 15; see further discussion below), officials are appointed, and for three months (i.e., from the first of the tenth month to the beginning of the first month) the commission met with the offending men (vv. 16-17).

"The Heavy Rain" (10:10)

As mentioned above, two reasons are given for the formation of this commission: (1) the serious character of the transgression, and (2) the heavy rain. How are we to understand this reference to the "rain"? On the one hand, it may be a simple historical reference. On the other hand, perhaps it is mentioned to underscore God's past and present faithfulness to the land which is so dependent on the rain. As the people gather to make a decision concerning obedience to the divine teaching, the rain, which falls so hard that they cannot stand in it, reminds them of the significance of their decision. According to Deut. 11:10-17, obedience to the commandments gives promise of rain and fertility, but to a disobedient people Yahweh will "shut up the heavens, so that there be no rain, and the land yield no fruit, and you perish quickly off the good land which the LORD gives you" (cf. Hag. 1:10-11).

81

Resistance to Reform (10:15)

Opposition to the action taken by Ezra and the community is noted in v. 15. We know almost nothing about the nature of this resistance. The four men mentioned are no doubt spokesmen for the families of which they are members, and possibly they are leaders of a much larger group that has taken exception to the viewpoint of the majority. The word "only" in the RSV should not be taken to mean "only these four men." The Hebrew term in the text (*'ak*) signifies an adversative (e.g., "but"). Concerning those who head up the opposition (namely, Jonathan and Jahzeiah), we have no information. Their names do not occur again in Ezra or Nehemiah. Those supporting them are Shabbethai the Levite and Meshullam. The former may be referred to in Neh. 8:7. Meshullam, which appears to be a popular name (see esp. Nehemiah), may be the one mentioned in Ezra 8:16. If so, he was considered to be a respected leader in the community. Another man with the name Meshullam is also mentioned in v. 29; he is one who had married a foreign wife. If he is the same one mentioned in v. 15, then we can understand his support of the opposition leaders. But we cannot be certain of these identifications.

The nature of the opposition referred to in v. 15 is also unknown to us. It is conceivable that it relates to the plan mentioned in v. 14 (cf. v. 16). More likely, the resistance has to do with the proposal that Jewish men separate from their foreign wives. In the past, these marriages had been accepted, or at least tolerated, in the community. Now mass divorce is commanded. Considering the severity of the action, one should not be surprised that some objected to it. The reference to the opposition has the character of a matter-of-fact statement. This is surprising. One would have expected a sharp rebuke aimed at this group.

MEN WHO HAVE MARRIED
FOREIGN WOMEN (10:18-44)

Those who know most intimately the relationship that God has with his people are also those who bear the most responsibility (cf. Amos 3:2 and 1 Pet. 4:17). Among the people of God, the priests are the privileged and honored leaders. One expects that they, who handle the divine oracles, will be living examples of God's way in the community. This expectation suffers some disappointment in Ezra's time, as it had in earlier periods (cf. Hos. 4:4-6; 5:1-2). Involved in marriage to foreign women are members of four priestly families (cf. Ezra 2:36-39). Included is the family of Jeshua, the son of Jozadak, the high priest who (with Zerubbabel) was pioneer leader among the returned exiles (Ezra 5:2) and who was held in high honor by Haggai and Zechariah.

Laxness concerning the commandments had seduced even those who were at the center of Jewish leadership. Now, finally, the priests "pledged themselves to put away their wives" and made a "guilt offering" (v. 19). A similar procedure was probably followed for the second- and third-level clergy (vv. 23-24) as well as for laypersons ("of Israel," vv. 25-43). The men who had married foreign wives numbered a little more than 110 persons (cf. the MT and LXX). Of this number seventeen were priests and ten were lower clergy — twenty-seven clergy in all.

Between the Lines: Tears (10:44)

The Hebrew of the second clause in v. 44 is not clear. Literally the full text reads: "And all these had taken foreign wives and there was from them (masc.) wives and they (masc.) put [bore?] children." It may be that the LXX represents what is intended by the MT: "All these had taken foreign wives and had borne children by them." If this is what the passage is saying, then the chapter ends with a touch of human feeling, that is, it recognizes what a tragic experience this will be — especially for the wives who had children. The RSV has adopted a reading from 1 Esd. 9:36. If this is an accurate reading of the text, then the book ends on a harsh note (see Ezra 10:3). No information is given concerning the care for those who have been set aside; one hopes that the reformers under the leadership of Ezra remembered the gentle words of the Torah that call for compassion as well as the hard commands that demand separation.

A COVENANT COMMUNITY LIVES BY ITS FAITHFULNESS

Habakkuk, the Book of Hebrews, and Ezra

In a time of oppression Habakkuk declares that "the righteous shall live by his *faithfulness*" (2:4; Heb. *'emunah;* see RSV mg). Traditionally, Christians have understood Habakkuk to be speaking of "faith" rather than "faithfulness." Paul's use of this passage in Rom. 1:17 and Gal. 3:11 has strengthened this view. But the context of Hab. 2:4 makes it clear that the prophet is speaking of faithfulness. Such is the meaning of this phrase in Heb. 10:38-39 also. This sense of faithfulness, however, is not foreign to Paul's use of the text. In the same letter in which he quotes Hab. 2:4 (Gal. 2:11), he has sharp words for those who try to live by faith but without faithfulness (Gal. 5; cf. Jas. 2:14-26). A community that dissociates "faith" too sharply from faithfulness stands in danger of dissolution.

Although the issues facing Ezra were quite different from those confronting Habakkuk and the author of Hebrews, there is similarity in emphasis. For all three, the times called for faithfulness — for holding fast to traditions that had given life to the community. Although faithfulness must be a continuing response of community members, in times of crisis and threat it receives special emphasis. Such is the case with the Jewish community after the Exile. While marriages with foreigners may have been tolerated in an earlier time, that kind of tolerance was too much to expect of the small Jewish community that was grasping for a future following the catastrophe of the Exile. These marriages were undercutting the foundations of the community. For this reason, Ezra and the Jewish leadership chose the drastic action of divorce; it was a decision *for* the community even though it must have caused deep pain for individuals and individual families.

Learning from Actions We Do Not Favor

Ezra's decision to bring about mass divorce from foreign women is not one that we favor today (contrast 1 Cor. 7:12-16). However, we need not agree with Ezra's approach in order to understand what was involved in that decision and to learn from it. A number of teachings in Scripture function in this way for us. For example, Paul's teaching that slaves should respect their masters (Eph. 6:5-8; Col. 3:22) does not mean that we should affirm slavery, but it may say something about how people should respond to employers. Jesus appears to have taught that there is no valid reason for divorce (Mark 10:10-12), except, possibly, for adultery (Matt. 5:31-32; 19:1-9). In a new situation, Paul reinterprets this teaching (1 Cor. 7:15), but in his discussion he emphasizes, as Jesus does, the importance of marriage. Although many Christians today have embraced a more liberal view of divorce, the teaching of Jesus and Paul continues to underscore for us the sacredness of the marriage bond.

Ezra's action also reminds us that marriage has implications for family, children, community, and faith. Those who participate in intermarriage are involving themselves not merely with the other person but with the interplay of primal forces and beliefs

84

that may be in conflict with each other (e.g., concerning the meaning of life and the shape of the future). If Ezra's "solution" was harsh and drastic, it was because the issue had to do with the continued life of the community of faith.

More than many realize, that issue is important to us today. Christian communities who have minority status in various parts of our world know how important it is to the life of the community to marry within the faith. V. Martin writes concerning the Christians of Dakar, Africa, who are a minority group living amidst a large population (370,000) of which 80% are Muslim: "Practically the whole of the Christian community intermarries (92 per cent)" (V. Martin, "Les Groupes Chritianises de Dakar," in *Christianity in Tropical Africa*, 362-97, esp. 395: English summary). No doubt this is the story in many parts of the world where a community feels pressure from without. The ideal of openness to others may not always be an option. *Sometimes preservation of a way of life dictates a policy which disappoints the democratic, ecumenical spirit.*

The Book of
NEHEMIAH

JERUSALEM IN RUINS
Nehemiah 1:1-11

COMFORT MY PEOPLE (1:1-4)

Nehemiah: "God Comforts"

"Comfort, comfort my people, says your God," are the opening words of the Prophet of the Exile (Isa. 40:1). These words and other oracles in Isa. 40 – 55 announce the return of the exiles to the land and the restoration of the Jewish community. None of the exilic prophets indicates *how* these people will return or *how* the community will be restored. The whole program of return and restoration appears at first sight to be completely the work of God. But an acquaintance with Israel's history, as well as our own, makes us aware that God does little without the help (!) of people.

We will better understand Second Isaiah's hope for the future if we read his prophecies together with the books of Ezra and Nehemiah. Further, the material in Ezra and Nehemiah will not appear to be so tedious if we read it in the light of Isa. 40 – 55, for then we will see that what is reported in these books stands in continuity with the great and glorious hopes of Second Isaiah.

God's promises for the future seldom come to pass unless some person "catches the vision" and works with God to bring the future to reality. Nehemiah was such a person; he caught the vision of a restored, secure Jewish community. The accident of his name underlines the biblical theme of God working out his plans in cooperation with people. Nehemiah's name means "God comforts." God "comforted" his people *through* the work of Nehemiah and, of course, others. The book of Ezra also emphasizes this theme.

"The Words of Amos . . . Jeremiah . . . Nehemiah" (1:1)

The book of Nehemiah opens with an unusual superscription for an historical narrative: "The words of Nehemiah." A number of prophetic books begin in this manner (e.g., Amos 1:1; Jer. 1:1; Mic. 1:1); whether intended or not, these opening words remind us of the prophetic character of Nehemiah's work. Although he is a layperson, he stands with the great prophets in interceding for his people and in calling them to be faithful to the Sinai covenant (see B.T. *Berakoth* 13a, where Nehemiah is called a "prophet"). He is never included among the prophets in the Hebrew Bible, but his "call" has a prophetic character to it.

The Call of Nehemiah and of Moses (1:2-4)

Nehemiah's brother (or a near-kinsman) reports to him on the difficult conditions in the land of Judah and tells him that the city walls still lie in ruins from the Babylonian debacle in 587 B.C.E. The Jewish community lies unprotected from the attacks and influence of groups that are unsympathetic to the teaching of the Mosaic covenant and to the community committed to this covenant. Unless action is taken, the ruined walls will be a symbol of what will happen to the people who live in this community; that is, the old teachings that have given them life and hope will have crumbled also, and the community, with its special character, will die.

The "burdens" of the Hebrews and the brutality directed against them were the "call" to action for Moses (a violent action but viewed as a just and a justified one in the Jewish tradition and in the NT; see, e.g., Exod. 2:11-15; *Midrash Rabbah* on Exod. 2:11-15; and Acts 7:23-29). No doubt other prophets also "heard" God calling to them because they were sensitive to some special need in the community (cf., e.g., Hag. 1:1-6). Similarly, a Jewish community lying in ruin and danger — on the edge of existence — constituted a "call" for Nehemiah. "Seeing" and "hearing" the *need* was an important part of God's call in the past; it is so today.

The comparison to Moses, by the way, does not end with the similarity relating to the "call" from God. In addition, like Moses, Nehemiah held a privileged position which protected him from personal suffering. His title of "cupbearer to the king" (1:11) in the Persian court does not seem to us to be a very exalted one, but such a person was a trusted and respected official — one who had close contact with the king and his family. Nehemiah could have continued living among the elite, but he left the good life, as did Moses, to share the sufferings of the Jewish community (cf. Heb. 11:23-26). He who "had it made" in life did not forget his own people (see also the story of Esther).

INTERCESSION (1:5-11)

Corporate and Individual Responsibility

Nehemiah's intercession on behalf of the Jewish community in the land underscores once more his kinship to Israel's prophets (see, e.g., Jer. 42:2-4). But he does not pray simply for *them;* he offers a prayer of repentance for himself and his family, for he sees himself as a participant in the sins of Israel. Of course, he himself did not actually have a part in the previous "sins of the people of Israel" (v. 6), because he was born among the exiles. But he is one with his people: what they have done, he has done; what they are, he is.

This concept of corporate solidarity should not be pressed so hard that it destroys individual responsibility, but it is a needed counterbalance to those Christian traditions which overemphasize individuality. In these later traditions, the corporate confession of sins (past and present) plays almost no part in worship. It is assumed that when church people have been involved in sinful acts (e.g., the oppression of the poor, blacks, and Jews) this only proves that they were not Christians — not part of the *true* Church. But to say this is to believe that only pure people really belong to the Church. But this cannot be true. We who take to ourselves the glory of the Church must also bear responsibility for its failures. That truth holds for all religious and political communities.

The Faithful God and Unfaithful Israel (1:5-10)

The prayer of confession is addressed to "the great and terrible God who keeps covenant and steadfast love with those who love him and keep his commandments" (v. 5). But, as Nehemiah admits, Israel *has not* shown true love for God and she *has not* kept the commandments (v. 7).

If Israel has behaved so unfaithfully, has Nehemiah any grounds for calling upon God? Yes! He knows that God is the one who forgives failure when people repent and return to a true and faithful covenant relationship. This is the word of "gospel" spoken to Moses (Deut. 30:1-4) — a word which opens the future for those who, together with Nehemiah, "have acted very corruptly" (v. 7; cf. Ps. 103:6-13). In company with Nehemiah are those (leaders?) in the community who are sincere in their desire to turn fully to Yahweh; they are the ones who now "delight to fear [i.e., to love or to be loyal to] the name" of Yahweh (v. 11). Observe that the terms "fear" *(yir'ah)* and "love" *('ahab)* often have

91

approximately the same meaning in the OT (see, e.g., Deut. 10:12).

Pleading for his people, Nehemiah does what Moses did when he interceded for the Israelites who sinned at the foot of Mt. Sinai; Nehemiah reminds God of his promise and observes that the people that are before him now are *his* people — the very ones he has "redeemed" from Egypt and Babylon (vv. 8-10; cf. Exod. 32:11-14). Nehemiah appears to be saying that it makes no sense at all to bring the exiles home and leave Judah in chaos. God guided *his* people out of captivity back to the land; should he not bring to completion this saving work by establishing them safely in Jerusalem behind secure walls? To Nehemiah, any other ending to the story is inconceivable.

"Give Success to Thy Servant" (1:11)

This plea underscores the divine-human partnership. Nehemiah has confessed the sins of the people (vv. 6-7) and believes that Yahweh will forgive his sinful people now that they have turned around and "delight to fear" him (vv. 9, 11). But that is not the end of it. How will God work in the lives of the Jews now that he has received them back? Nehemiah knows that someone must represent God on this earth and must do, in fact, what God wants done. Nehemiah views himself as the one who must be God's representative. He prays for "success" *(tsalah)* as he goes to speak to "this man" (i.e., the Persian king, Artaxerxes I). Instead of "this man," one would expect "King Artaxerxes" or "the Persian ruler." By means of this phrase, Nehemiah may be saying that even though the king is the very powerful ruler of Persia, he is only a mortal man (see F. C. Fensham, *Ezra and Nehemiah*, 157). God is stronger and wiser; he will prevail.

The Servant of God and Goliaths

The above interpretation of the phrase (i.e., "this man") is possibly correct. Whether this view of the matter is true or not, however, its occurrence in Nehemiah recalls other passages in the Bible in which we are reminded of the frail, human character of those who *seem* to be invincible (Isa. 31:1-3), who take on the affectations of a divine being (Isa. 14:3-17). The words of the young David to the Philistine giant have the same significance: "You come to me with a sword and with a spear and with a javelin, but I come to you in the name of the LORD of hosts" (1 Sam. 17:45). Often we let the Goliaths of this world get by with their pretensions of being more than what they are: human beings.

Belief in the God of Abraham and Moses does, at least, three things for us: (1) It prevents one from being drawn into acceptance of the divine pretensions of the powerful (see how Daniel, Joseph, and Nehemiah respect the foreign rulers yet keep their identity as people of God). (2) It keeps alive hope for the surprises of history because God's plans often overrule those made by people — even kings (Prov. 8:15-16; Isa. 10:6-19). (3) It renews the inner vitality so that the weak become strong (cf. Isa. 40:29 and Josh. 1:9). In the court of the Persian king, Nehemiah observed the royal courtesies ("if it pleases the king, and if your servant has found favor in your sight," 2:5), but, in reality, Nehemiah knows that this king stands under the kingship of God and is but flesh and blood — a creature created by God.

Effective Speech

Nehemiah prays that Yahweh will "grant him mercy" (i.e., divine favor) when he goes in to see "this man." He hopes that Artaxerxes will seriously consider his request to leave the royal service in order to serve Yahweh, that is, to bring order and security to Yahweh's people in the land of Israel. If the Persian government had recently halted the rebuilding of the walls of Jerusalem, as some scholars believe, because it feared that work on them constituted rebellious activity (cf. Ezra 4:7-23), then it is not likely that the Persian king would be sympathetic to Nehemiah's request. In any case, Nehemiah prays that God will give him success in securing the support of the king for his planned trip to Jerusalem.

The right words, the right approach must be used; untactful speech or any alienating behavior could result in the king opposing Nehemiah's plans. Nehemiah prays that God will give him "success," that is, help him to make effective use of his resources so that he will be as skillful as possible in making his presentation before the king. This understanding of Nehemiah's prayer to God appears to be confirmed by Neh. 2:4. In this passage, Nehemiah is standing before the king and the king asks him: "For what do you make request?" Before Nehemiah responds, he prays to God so that, presumably, he will be successful in what he says.

God and the Wise Person

God is with the "wise" person — with those who give serious thought to action, who understand that words and actions have implications. Wisdom literature often contrasts the "wise" and the "foolish." These terms have little to do with formal education;

they relate to using one's head, understanding how life runs. The "wise" person is one who gives careful thought to his speech (Prov. 16:23). Proverbs 22:11 observes that the one who is pure in heart and *"whose speech is gracious, will have the king as his friend."* In contrast, the "fool" gives no thought to his speech and action; he "babbles" (Prov. 10:14), "throws off restraint" (Prov. 14:16), "takes no pleasure in understanding" (Prov. 18:2), and finally brings ruin upon himself. The Bible emphasizes that lasting success can never be had without the help of God, but it is equally insistent that people are not passive receptacles who are pushed around by God. God's servants are expected to use all the resources they have to accomplish their service for him. See our discussion in the next chapter concerning the careful thought that lay behind Nehemiah's plans.

FROM PALACE LIFE TO
JERUSALEM'S RUINS
Nehemiah 2:1-20

GOD IS WITH THE WISE (2:1-9)

Success Comes to Those Who Plan Ahead

Four months after receiving sad news concerning the walls of Jerusalem (i.e., from the month of Kislev to Nisan; cf. Neh. 1:1 and 2:1), Nehemiah initiates a plan to secure the support of the Persian king for a rebuilding program. That he waited such a long time to act may reflect the delicate nature of his request for the king's help. As we have already noted, Ezra 4:12-16 reports that King Artaxerxes had issued a decree which ordered work on the city walls to be stopped. If this Artaxerxes was the same king whom Nehemiah served in the court (i.e., Artaxerxes I, who ruled from 465 to 424), then we can understand Nehemiah's delay. In such a context, one must lay plans carefully — and wait for the right occasion — before approaching the king on this controversial subject. Other examples of careful preparation come to mind: the planning of Esther as she seeks to save her people (Esth. 5 – 7); Naomi's suggestion to Ruth about securing the assistance of Boaz (Ruth 3); the discussion between Bathsheba and Nathan about an effective approach to David so that Solomon would be appointed king (1 Kgs. 1:1-38).

In Nehemiah's venture to secure Jerusalem, success requires the help of God, *but it also demands that Nehemiah be a wise person.* This is not the time to operate "off the top of the head"; in such cases even God might not be able to help. Nehemiah is seeking the help of the king of Persia, who may already be suspicious of the Jewish interest in rebuilding the walls of Jerusalem. If he is not approached in the right way or at the right time he could respond with an angry no — a disaster for the Jewish community and for Nehemiah (cf. Prov. 20:2). It is the wise person who recognizes this fact and therefore moves with caution.

The Right Time (2:1)

Nehemiah waits until a time of celebration before he puts his "plan" into action. He decides that *this time* of happiness and drinking is also the time for action on his part (v. 1; cf. Ruth 3:1-5 regarding Naomi's advice that Ruth seek Boaz during the harvest time when he was drinking). In his previous service to the king Nehemiah had always entered into the spirit of the festivals; never before had he reflected any sadness that resulted from personal problems — a point that the text underscores (v. 1). The king, who must have known his "cupbearer" well, asks him the cause of his sadness (v. 2). Did Nehemiah intend the king to notice his sadness? One cannot be certain, but it is likely that he did (see Derek Kidner, *Ezra and Nehemiah*, 80, who also suggests this possibility). The king, so Nehemiah may have thought, will surely ask him the reason for his sadness, and this will give him a chance to reply and test the king's mood before he makes his request.

The Right Words (2:2-5)

The king *does* question him about his sadness, and Nehemiah reports: "Then I was very much afraid" (v. 2). Perhaps he was afraid because, now that he had the ear of the king, he realized how much depended on what he would say. Finally, he tells the king that the ruins of Jerusalem weigh heavily on his heart. So far so good. But the king moves to the crucial question: "For what do you make request?" (v. 4). Another tension point is reached, and, before answering, Nehemiah prays to God — apparently seeking his guidance and help in responding to the king. Nehemiah has already prayed to God and made his plans (1:11), so this prayer is not a frantic call for God to "take over." Rather it is a final "turning of the mind" to God — on the spot — before making the crucial request.

Finally, he addresses the king and requests that he be sent to Judah to rebuild the city where his fathers are buried. Artaxerxes surely must know that he is speaking of Jerusalem (i.e., this city on whose walls he had earlier forbidden further work), but Nehemiah never mentions the name of the city. Is the name of Jerusalem missing only by chance or is its absence another sign of Nehemiah's delicate, careful diplomacy? The oblique language used by diplomats (even in our present day) when speaking about situations of which both parties are informed points in favor of the latter position (see Jacob Myers, *Ezra. Nehemiah*, 99).

The King Says Yes (2:6-9)

The king responded favorably to Nehemiah, thus reversing the decree recorded in Ezra 4:17-22. We are not told why the king *now* allowed the rebuilding to continue. Perhaps the new decision is due to a number of reasons. It has been suggested that trouble in the empire may have persuaded the king to give consideration to a program that would help pacify the Palestinian region (see John Bright, *History,* 380). The personal regard that the king and queen (see 2:6) had for Nehemiah and the Jewish community may also have played a part in this happy turnabout.

Surprisingly, the king's decision does not appear to be a grudging permission. At the request of Nehemiah, he provided letters of introduction that would bring him the cooperation of Persian governors (v. 7) and other important persons (v. 8). In addition, the king sent a military escort to protect Nehemiah and those accompanying him. Besides giving protection to Nehemiah, this escort also was a signal "to whom it may concern" that Nehemiah had the ear of the king.

Not too much should be made of the fact that Nehemiah accepted military protection which Ezra had refused (Ezra 8:22). First, Ezra rejected military protection because he had made a point of saying that *God* would be his protection. Nehemiah apparently had not done this. It may be important to observe also that Ezra was a priest and may have believed that his priestly position necessitated the trusting action recorded in Ezra 8:22. Nehemiah was a layperson, sent by Artaxerxes to be governor over the land of Judah (Neh. 5:14). It would be most appropriate and wise for Nehemiah, as an official of the Persian government, to continue what was probably a customary policy (see F. C. Fensham, *Ezra and Nehemiah,* 177). Further, serving God does not always mean forsaking the assistance of the government — even though such help has sometimes opened the community of faith to ruinous governmental influence.

THE OPPOSITION (2:10-20)

Jesus "went about doing good" (Acts 10:38), but he had enemies because the "good" he did was not what some people wanted. This is the story of Nehemiah's life also. He came seeking the "welfare" (*tobah,* "good") of the Jews, but his mission came as a disturbance to three influential leaders: "Sanballat the Horonite," "Tobiah the servant, the Ammonite" (2:10, 19), and "Geshem the Arab." Our knowledge concerning these three men is minimal.

97

Sanballat

The Jews of Elephantine in Egypt sent an Aramaic letter (dated ca. 410 B.C.E.) to Jerusalem seeking help in the rebuilding of their temple. This letter indicates that a similar letter had been sent to "Delaiah and Shelemiah, the sons of Sanballat the governor of Samaria" (*ANET,* 492, line 29). If the Sanballat mentioned in this text is the same one referred to in Nehemiah (as most scholars believe), then, as governor of Samaria, he was a formidable opponent. No doubt he saw Nehemiah's visit to Jerusalem as a mission which would produce a strong Jerusalem and therefore bring about a lessening of his own political power.

We know nothing of the character of Sanballat. The last three letters in the names of his sons (Delaiah and Shelemiah) reflect the Hebrew syllable *yah,* which is a short form of Yahweh. This fact may indicate that he was "in some way" a believer in Yahweh. It does not, however, give us any indication of the character of his own personal belief, because the Jewish community in Elephantine also believed in Yahweh but it was a faith far removed from that held in Jerusalem (e.g., they represented Yahweh as having a consort). Sanballat is not presented as an enemy of the religious community at Jerusalem; his opposition is limited to the strengthening of the security of the city. But in Sanballat's opposition to the Jews, we see renewed the old hostility between the north (Samaria) and the south (Judah).

Tobiah

Another official who took a stand against Nehemiah's mission was Tobiah. Although his name means "Yahweh is my good," this did not stop him from opposing the "good" (v. 10) that Nehemiah sought for the city of Jerusalem. Tobiah was probably a rather important official in the Persian empire (*'ebed,* "servant," may have this meaning). He is called "the Ammonite," but this does not necessarily mean that he *was* an Ammonite by birth; most likely this designation speaks of his area of service (i.e., Ammonite territory) to the Persian government. Ancient texts speak of a Tobiah family that served in the government of Ptolemy II (285-246 B.C.E.; see John Bright, *History,* 414). It is possible that this family is a descendant of the civil servant, Tobiah, who is mentioned here in Nehemiah.

Geshem

The third opponent of Nehemiah was "Geshem the Arab" (v. 19; cf. Neh. 6:6). The information concerning him is also tenuous.

He is often identified with a Geshem who was "a powerful chieftain of Qedar (Dedan) in northwestern Arabia"; his rule appears to have covered a wide area, including the southern part of Judah (John Bright, *History,* 382). If this identification is correct, then Nehemiah had powerful enemies to the north, south, and east. True, he had the support of King Artaxerxes, but being far removed from the court of the Persian king, Nehemiah was vulnerable to all kinds of roadblocking actions by people like Sanballat, Tobiah, and Geshem.

Secrecy: Be Wise As Serpents (2:11-16)

No doubt it was this strong opposition to his coming that caused Nehemiah to survey the city in secret — by night. Only a select group of people knew of these hidden, night tours when Nehemiah inspected the ruins of the city and estimated what could and should be done. Even leaders in the Jewish community were unaware of what he was doing (v. 16). The reason for the secrecy was, probably, to keep the opposition ignorant of his plans. There is a time to confront directly the opposition (e.g., Esth. 7:1-6) and a time to be secretive (Esth. 5:1-8) or evasive (Mark 11:27-33). Jesus urged his disciples, when in the midst of hostile people, to be "wise as serpents and innocent as doves" (Matt. 10:16; cf. Jer. 38:14-28). One may wish to be an open person, but such openness should not be a naivete that plays into the hands of the opposition. The day is coming, Nehemiah knows, when he must take his stand, but (to the degree possible) he wants to select this time for himself.

The Opposition: Are You Planning to Rebel? (2:17-19)

Following his inspection, Nehemiah calls the people together, places before them the sorry state of the city that once "was a princess among the cities" (Lam. 1:1), and rallies them to action. He reminds them of God's guidance in this whole affair *and* the support which the king has promised (v. 18). They accept his leadership and indicate that they are ready to begin the difficult task of rebuilding (vv. 17-18). But the three adversaries (and those who support them) are present also. The old charge is aired one more time: "Are you rebelling against the king?" (v. 19). It was this accusation that halted an earlier attempt at rebuilding the walls (Ezra 4:11-24). True, Nehemiah had received permission from King Artaxerxes to rebuild the walls of Jerusalem; therefore, one assumes that the king was persuaded that the earlier accusations were not true. But continued repetition of this charge by a significant number of people (or a number of significant people!) could make the king uneasy once again and bring about another decree which would stop the work.

It is possible, of course, that these charges were *not* created out of thin air. We can imagine that some people in this new community must have seen the rebuilding project as a freedom movement — a movement that would bring about the restoration of the nation. Certainly some people must have looked forward to release from the Persian overlord (see, e.g., the hopes that Haggai and Zechariah had in Zerubbabel). What may have been a "big lie" concerning *Nehemiah's intentions* could have been close to the truth of what *some people wanted*. For further comments concerning the political significance of Nehemiah in the restored community (i.e., was he a descendant of David?!), see our comments in ch. 6.

Sometimes people who support a leader-reformer undercut such leadership by making extreme statements about what this leader is planning to do. Was that the situation in regard to Jesus also (cf. Mark 10:37; Acts 1:6; 3:19-21)? It may have been a problem with which Nehemiah had to contend. It is hard enough to deal with a suspicious overlord when one is completely innocent; the difficulty increases immeasurably when one must not only answer to a shadowed past (i.e., Jerusalem *was* a rebellious city) but also deal with "friends" who have revolution on their minds and thus misrepresent the cause. As a leader of a city that has a "past" and supported by friends who speak carelessly, Nehemiah was in a position where even the best actions can be misinterpreted.

Further, it is not easy to dissociate oneself from past actions and from present rumors (in the matter of rebellion) *when one is working hard to build the defenses of the city!* If we take a generous view of Nehemiah's opponents for a moment (i.e., assume that they are not completely evil — few people are), we may be able to understand their response to Nehemiah. How did they know, for certain, that this Jewish community was building the defenses of the city only to defend themselves from marauders? The possibility existed that they were preparing to rebel — seeking power that will threaten surrounding communities. This is the situation in our modern era with regard to world peace. The Superpowers always speak in terms of defense as they strengthen their military capability, but the world is in fear because it is difficult to distinguish between defensive and offensive weapons.

Confrontation (2:20)

Nehemiah sweeps aside what he considers to be false charges. Although he may have felt anxious before his adversaries, his twofold response to them is a bold one (v. 20). He declares that God is with the Jews and will make them "prosper." This trust in God is not simply blind faith; it builds on what has already happened, that is, the king's support of the building project. Further, Nehemiah rejects the three troublemakers as outsiders. They have no real part ("portion"), no legal "right" *(tsedaqah)* in the Jewish community. They are not part of the tradition (see RSV "memorial"); they are outsiders.

These adversaries are "displeased" that Nehemiah has arrived to promote the "welfare" (i.e., the good; Heb. *tobah*) of the Israelites in the city (v. 10). Because they are not a part of the community, they do not really care about it. They are angry, however, that Nehemiah has come seeking its "welfare" (i.e., "the good"), because his assertive action is obstructing the "good" they are seeking for themselves. On the one hand, as we have indicated, they are perhaps worried about the "balance of power" in that area. On the other hand, it may be that they wish to deny secure "living space" to the Jewish community so that they may have control. If the latter is true, then the spirit of Sanballat, Tobiah, and Geshem continues to live in our day — on the individual and community levels. Looking out for ourselves (i.e., our good) — which often means seeking an advantage — sometimes blinds us to the right that other people have in seeking their good.

WORKING TOGETHER TO REBUILD THE WALL

Nehemiah 3:1-32

A "DETAILED" SUMMARY

With the beginning of ch. 3, we are already in the midst of the building activities that will eventually provide a wall of protection around the city of Jerusalem. We are not told how Nehemiah recruited or appointed the workers. Those are details that are not important to the compiler of this material. He gives us only what he judges to be necessary information. The following passage (vv. 1-32) appears to be rather detailed, but, of course, it does not tell the complete story about the rebuilding of the walls. It is a "detailed" summary of this important event.

The Priests Work "next to" Laypersons (3:1-2)

Chapter 2 ended with Nehemiah fending off his opponents. In the following verses, with one exception (v. 5), we have a listing of those who supported Nehemiah in his vision of a rebuilt Jerusalem. At the head of the list stands the high priest, Eliashib. He was the grandson of Jeshua (Neh. 12:10), who himself was the high priest during the period of Zerubbabel's activity (Ezra 2:2; 5:2). Jeshua's concern for Jerusalem was carried on, therefore, by his grandson.

Eliashib and the priests did not simply oversee the work; they themselves, under the direction of a lay administrator, actually worked on the walls. Together with other workers, they "built" (see, e.g., 3:1, 2) the walls. Their task was the Sheep Gate, which (probably) was assigned to them because it stood nearest the temple.

The priests under Eliashib embrace a commonsense theology. In the temple worship, they celebrated God's help and protection (possibly reading Psalms such as Ps. 46), but they knew that one cannot leave everything to God. God's promise of protection does not mean that people should neglect to protect themselves and the "lifegiving" traditions of their community. God is *with* his people; he does not substitute *for* them. He is *with* those who use all of their resources to achieve success and fulfillment.

Eliashib must have hoped for a time when spears would be turned into pruning hooks (Isa. 2:4), when Jerusalem would be able to rest secure without walls for defense (Zech. 2:4ff. and Ezek. 38:10-23), but, in his judgment and in the judgment of those listed in these verses, that time had not arrived. In Nehemiah, as in the OT generally, defense against the enemy is not viewed as a contradiction of trust in God (see our further discussion in ch. 4).

Working Together

A variety of people from Jerusalem gave themselves to the task of rebuilding: priests (v. 1), Levites (v. 17), goldsmiths and perfumers (v. 8), officials (vv. 9, 12), and merchants (v. 32). The list conveys wholehearted commitment on the part of Jerusalem's citizens. There is a special note that Shallum "and his daughters" (v. 12) also worked on the walls. This comment speaks of the special enthusiasm of this family because, usually, only men were expected to do such work.

One might expect the people of Jerusalem to take part in this project because it had to do with their own safety. But they were not alone in this work. People from other communities also gave themselves to the task, for example, people from Jericho (v. 2), Tekoah (v. 5), Gibeon (v. 7), Zanoah (v. 13), and Beth-haccherem (v. 14), as well as other places. Even the son of the ruler of Mizpah contributed his strength (v. 19; cf. v. 7). The commitment of the citizens of Tekoa is exceptional. They worked on *two* sections of the wall (vv. 5, 27)!

Some Refused to Work (3:5)

The "nobles" of Tekoa, however, "did not put their necks to the work of their Lord" (v. 5). The Hebrew term translated "their Lord" *('adonehem)* is an ambiguous expression and could also be translated "their lords" or "their lord." We favor the latter suggestion and believe the reference is to Nehemiah, the governor (cf. Ezra 10:3). No information is given to explain why these nobles refused to cooperate. It is possible that, as members of the upper class, they had established business or personal friendships with the non-Jews of the surrounding territory (cf. Neh. 6:17-19). If so, they may have believed that the building of a wall was an unwise, provocative act on the part of the Jews — an act that would only increase hostility. Or possibly they worried about reprisals if they contributed to Jerusalem's defense. F. C. Fensham (*Ezra and Nehemiah,* 174) has noted that Tekoa was exposed to the attack of one of Nehemiah's enemies, Geshem the Arab. This fact makes one all the more appreciative of the citizenry of Tekoa who, despite the danger of retaliation, worked willingly for the defense of Jerusalem. Other groups may have worked for the safety of Jerusalem under the same threatening circumstances. They were willing to endure danger to themselves in order to create some security for other members of the Jewish community. These people are kin to the tribesmen of Zebulun who "jeoparded their lives to the death" following Deborah into battle against Sisera (Judg. 5:18).

"Bear One Another's Burdens"

Helping others when it is convenient or even rewarding should not be despised, but risking one's own comfort and security to assist others deserves special praise. In the life of Israel the names of Moses (Exod. 2:11-19) and Jeremiah (Jer. 34:8-22) come to mind. Prisca and Aquila belong to this company of people also. Paul speaks of them as those "who risked their necks for my life" (Rom. 16:4; cf. Phil. 2:25-30).

If one is simply reading the Bible a chapter a day, this list of names in Neh. 3 may not prove very interesting. But if one reads this list with an eye to human hardship and the sacrifice endured for the sake of other people, it breaks the time barrier and speaks of those who today risk their lives and reputations for the good of others. Read in this way, this chapter also is a call to people of faith to heed the words of Paul: "Let no one seek [only!] his own good, but the good of his neighbor" (1 Cor. 10:24; cf. Gal. 6:2). Paul includes this injunction in a specific context, but this theme is central to both the OT and the NT and is applicable to all areas of life.

WITH HARD WORK, WEAPONS, AND THE HELP OF GOD
Nehemiah 4:1-23

THREAT AND RIDICULE (4:1-3)

The sounds of men and women working on the ruined walls of Jerusalem was a call to action for the enemies of the Jews. Enraged, Sanballat assembles his "army" (v. 2; NEB "garrison") as a show of force to threaten those supporting Nehemiah. Both Sanballat and Tobiah ridicule the efforts of those amateurs who are working so hard on the ruins (vv. 2-3). They have no idea how hard their task is. Further, some of the workmanship is laughable; Tobiah remarks that even a fox running on the wall would cave in parts of it (v. 3). His smirking comment may have had some basis in fact.

"HEAR, O OUR GOD" (4:4-5)

As Nehemiah tells the story of the difficulties he had in bringing about the rebuilding of the walls, the painful conflicts of the past move upon him again. Those past events will not remain in the past. He remembers the cutting words and the humiliating questions of his opponents (vv. 2-3). In addition, he cannot forget his own anguished cry that God would turn his enemies' cruelty back on themselves and bring them to ruin (v. 4).

Vengeance: The Cry of the Victim (4:5)

The fierceness of v. 5 may startle the reader: "Do not cover their guilt, and let not their sin be blotted out from thy sight" (cf. Jer. 18:23). With these words, Nehemiah pleads that the malicious acts against the Jews not be allowed to fade quietly into the past and be forgotten. Let there be no easy "forgive and forget" response to those who have caused so much pain to a struggling community. In these words, Nehemiah is asking God to remem-

105

ber the *victims* of these cruel acts. The pain that the Jews suffered from their enemies would now be more than doubled if there was not the hope that some day God would call these oppressors to account for their wickedness.

The Bible depicts God as gracious and forgiving, but this view of the divine Lord does not mean that he advertises "cheap grace" or "quick and easy forgiveness." God has an ear and a heart for those who suffer — for the victims. He holds oppressors responsible and will bring them to judgment. "Forgiveness" that quickly assures the oppressor that God will forgive has no sense of the victim's hurt; it is uncaring and cruel.

The Cry of Vengeance Is a Cry for Justice

Nehemiah believes in a God who cares. He prays for vindication; he calls for justice. This plea does not fall from his lips because he is a "hothead" who explodes into violent language at the slightest provocation. His anger grows out of long-term suffering; it rises from facing unyielding, unprincipled opponents who (as he understands it) want to destroy his work for God. It is this persistent, perverse hostility that also roused Jeremiah to a cry for vengeance (Jer. 18:18-23).

The call for God to avenge the cruelty done to his people is not limited to the OT. In Rom. 12:19-21, Paul declares that one should not avenge oneself because vengeance belongs to God. This is, in fact, the belief of Nehemiah and Jeremiah; they call upon God to take vengeance. They ask no more than the martyrs suffering persecution under the Romans (Rev. 6:10; 19:2). One is reminded also of the words of Jesus in Matt. 23. These strong words are a response to a blind, fanatical opposition on the part of some Pharisees (see, e.g., Matt. 23; cf. Mark 3:1-6). According to the present text of Matt. 23 (quite likely it was expanded by an editor who reflected the thinking of the early church), Jesus believes that the deeds of these people deserve the judgment that is coming (Matt. 23:33-38). This judgment is vindication for those whom these religious leaders have assaulted.

GOD FIGHTS AND WE FIGHT (4:6-20)

Nehemiah's Success Renews Enemy Anger (4:6-8)

In spite of threat and ridicule, under Nehemiah's leadership the Jews worked hard on the wall. They encircled the city completely with a wall that was "to half its height." The Hebrew phrase translated "to half its height" is somewhat ambiguous, but it probably means the wall was approximately half of its projected height.

The unexpected success of these inexperienced workers fires the anger of Sanballat and others who oppose the Jews. We learn now, by the way, that the leaders of Ashdod are part of the conspiracy against the Jews. This means that the Jewish community is completely surrounded by enemies: Ashdod (east, on the Phoenician coast); Ammon (west, in the Transjordan); Sanballat of Samaria (north), and Geshem the Arab (south and southwest).

Praying to God but Ready to Fight (4:9-14)

The threat of these enemies (vv. 11-12) in addition to the despair caused by the difficult work (v. 10) was almost too much to bear. But Nehemiah does not give up, nor does he let the workers surrender to fear or tiredness. Upon learning of an enemy plan to attack Jerusalem (v. 8), he, together with other Jews, prayed to God and "set a guard as a protection against them *day and night*" (v. 9). Nehemiah's precaution in setting up a guard "day and night" represents no rejection of the Exodus God who went before the fleeing Israelites "by day and by night" (Exod. 13:21-22). In that ancient flight, the Israelites were not simply passive pawns moved about by Yahweh; no, they went out "equipped for battle" (Exod. 13:18). Nehemiah faced the enemies of his day in the same way that Moses and Joshua faced those that confronted them, that is, with a belief that God fought *along with* his people.

God "with" us is no substitute for being watchful and strong in the face of danger. In this time of crisis, Nehemiah reminds the Jews that their God is "great and terrible" (v. 14) — one who "will fight for us" (v. 20). These words, however, are not intended to encourage a "leave it to God" attitude. Rather they are words that inspire courage to "fight for your brethren, your sons, your daughters, your wives, and your homes" (v. 14). In preparation for battle, Nehemiah had stationed people with weapons (swords, spears, and bows) at the places where he expected an attack (v. 13). But the attack did not come, because: (1) the enemies of the Jews became aware that the Jews knew about their plans and were prepared to fight; (2) "God had frustrated their plan" (v. 15). We should not try to separate these reasons from each other — they overlap. To Nehemiah both the divine and human actions explain the failure of the enemy to attack.

107

DEFENSE PLANS: UNPLEASANT BUT NECESSARY
(4:21-23)

The failure of Sanballat and his allies to attack gave the Jews a welcome reprieve. But Nehemiah did not relax; knowing that a later attack was possible, he organized and armed his people for defense (vv. 16-23). It is not a pleasant experience to strap on or hold weapons that may bring death to someone, but the alternative is not attractive either. There are times, perhaps, when the paths of non-resistance or passive resistance represent wise choices, but, unfortunately, in our kind of world (whether ancient or modern), these choices sometimes guarantee the destruction of the righteous. Weakness often invites attack, and frequently it is the weak who suffer harm. Nehemiah is not guilty of putting his trust in weapons rather than in Yahweh. He looks to God for strength and support, but he brings his people out "equipped for battle," like the ancient Israelites (Exod. 13:18).

INTERNAL PROBLEMS
Nehemiah 5:1-19

A NEW DANGER (5:1-5)

The preceding chapter depicted the citizens of Jerusalem as an armed camp, hard at work on a wall that would protect them from their hostile, non-Jewish neighbors. But some Jews in the city faced adversaries for which walls and weapons were no defense. These poor Jews were kept on the edge of poverty by greedy people within the Jewish community itself. In desperation, they cry out "against their Jewish brethren" (v. 1). Verses 2-5 describe their difficult circumstances. To survive means borrowing money, but in order to secure the loan one must offer one's property for collateral (vv. 3-4). For those who are very poor, the collateral has to be their children (v. 5).

What Does It Mean to Be in the Covenant Community?

Some biblical texts note that lazy people often do not succeed in life (e.g., Prov. 6:9-11; 20:4). However, other texts note that some people have a hard time in life because they are oppressed by the powerful and rich (e.g., Prov. 22:16; cf. 28:6). It is the latter case that applies here. Hard-working farmers have been hit by misfortune; with a little assistance they would be able to overcome their difficulty. But the people to whom they go for help are committed businessmen. Their motto is, "business is business," no matter whom they hurt. This purely business attitude stuns the poor farmers. How could "their Jewish brethren" (v. 1) so readily take advantage of them? They say: "Now our flesh is as the flesh of our brethren; our children are as their children" (v. 5). These words do not mean simply that the poor share a common humanity with the rich; it indicates also their oneness in the covenant relationship. The irony is painful. Some Jews who have come to the land from places of slavery (e.g., Babylon) meet further oppression in the covenant community of their homeland.

NEHEMIAH: THE EMANCIPATOR (5:6-13)

The Cry for Help (5:6)

Long before the time of Nehemiah, Yahweh (*and* Moses) heard the "cry" (from *za'aq*) of the Hebrews who were oppressed *in Egypt* (Exod. 2:23; 3:7). This "outcry" is heard again in the post-exilic period, but this time it comes from *inside the borders of Israel*. Nehemiah hears this "outcry" (v. 6; cf. v. 1) and is angry at this betrayal of the covenant; he takes action against the offenders. They have closed their ears to the teaching of the covenant and have become oppressors.

Nehemiah knows that a community that approves (or is silent before) this oppressive attitude of the rich cannot be a true community of Yahweh (vv. 7, 9), because Yahweh's Torah forbids taking advantage of the weak and poor. According to the Torah, no interest was to be taken for loans to members of the Israelite community (Exod. 22:25; Lev. 25:35-38; Deut. 15:7-11), and, if collateral was demanded for such loans, they were subject to certain humane restrictions (Deut. 24:10-13). The relationship of Israelites to each other is supposed to reflect the gracious character of Yahweh revealed in the Exodus (Lev. 25:38).

Confronting a Legal but Immoral Activity (5:7-8)

In his summary of the situation, Nehemiah declares that he "brought charges against the nobles and the officials" (v. 7). Before a "great assembly" (v. 7), he accuses them of betraying the elemental standards of the covenant community: they have enslaved poor Jews and sold them to non-Jewish neighbors (v. 8). In his accusation before the "great assembly" (v. 7), Nehemiah mentions that he had established a program to redeem Jews who were enslaved by foreigners. As money was available, the community leaders would purchase the freedom of these Jews from their foreign masters and restore them as free men to the Jewish community. However, the rich nobles worked counter to this kind of humane action; the Jews who were enslaved to them they sold in turn to foreigners. This meant that the Jewish community was forced to buy them back. The NEB, with an emendation of the text ("bought back by us" over against the RSV "sold to us") makes this sense of the passage clearer. For a different interpretation see F. C. Fensham, *Ezra and Nehemiah*, 194.

Seek the Good (5:9)

The silence of the nobles (v. 8) constitutes an admission that their actions were shameful — a violation of basic covenantal relation-

110

ships. Nehemiah declares that what they have done is "not good" (*lo'-tob;* v. 9); they have taken advantage of their weaker neighbors. Like certain Israelites of the 8th century they need to hear the words of Amos: "Seek good *[tob]* and not evil, that you may live, and so the LORD, the God of hosts, will be with you" (Amos 5:14).

It is the doing of the "good" (which centers on dealing with others according to justice and kindness) that pleases God. Standing in the tradition of the prophets and later Jewish teachers, Jesus has left us an example of how we are to relate to others. In the midst of a highly "theological" passage (Acts 10:34-43), it is striking to see a "practical" aspect of Jesus' ministry remembered: "he went about doing good and healing all that were oppressed by the devil, for God was with him" (Acts 10:38). The stories in the Gospels that speak of the relationship of Jesus to people are a commentary on the meaning of the word "good." We do not often emphasize the fact that Jesus "went about doing good" because we want to say more important (!) things about him. To declare that he did the "good" seems to demean him. We think we can cut corners on the "good" because God is concerned about bigger issues, but this God who is concerned about the "bigger issues" is more the God we have created than the God who created us.

What You Do Speaks Louder Than Your Words

The oppressive behavior of the nobles not only causes suffering to the poor in the community, it also opens up the community to ridicule from non-Jews (v. 9). Yahweh counted on Israel to be his witness (Isa. 43:12; 44:8) before the nations. The nobles *are* witnesses, but their actions prove that they are *false* witnesses. Their delight is not in "the law of the LORD" (Ps. 1:1-2); they are ruining the reputation of Yahweh.

Nehemiah is calling for community integrity. He is saying: "Let us be who we are. Should people oppose us and our God, let them oppose us because we are really different. Let us not, by our way of life, give to our enemies the opportunity to ridicule Yahweh's community." The continued presence of those who *say* they belong to the community of faith (they say: "Lord, Lord"; see Matt. 7:21-23) but in fact live for themselves provides ammunition even today for attacks on the Church and Synagogue.

Nehemiah (!) Is Part of the Problem (5:10)

While attacking the nobles (vv. 6-7), Nehemiah admits that even "I and my brethren and my servants are lending them [i.e., the

111

poor] money and grain" (v. 10). We should not think that Nehemiah was intentionally involved in oppressive religious practices, for such is not his character (see Neh. 5:14-19). Nevertheless, he was involved in the general practice of lending which apparently required collateral (also interest?) of the poor. Nehemiah, the social critic, was not fully free of guilt.

Such an admission comes as a surprise. It is often difficult for a reformer to admit participation in the sins of the community. When the oppressed were relatively silent, Nehemiah did what others did — only, perhaps, with a more generous spirit. Possibly the "outcry" (5:1, 6) of the poor brought home to him the harmful character of this policy. Nowhere does Nehemiah admit (or accuse others of) taking part in illegal procedure. He is opposing legal actions which in this special context are insensitive and immoral. They are actions that have no heart for people who are losing out in life.

The Nobles Finally (!) Agree to Help the Poor (5:10-13)

Nehemiah calls together a meeting ("assembly," v. 7; cf. v. 13) of the community and urges the rich (including himself and those allied with him) to forgive the debts of the poor farmers (v. 11). The nobles had been "silent" (v. 8) when Nehemiah had accused them of selling the poor debtors into slavery, but now, when Nehemiah asks them to forgo interest payments and to restore those things (e.g., lands and houses) that the poor have mortgaged, they agree to do it (v. 12).

Nehemiah now addresses the priests and has these religious leaders administer an oath to the nobles that they will do what they have "promised" to do (v. 12). The RSV translation of v. 12 conveys the idea that the priests were required to take an oath that they (i.e., the priests) would do what Nehemiah asked. The sentence in Hebrew is ambiguous, but we believe that the "them" in v. 12 refers to the nobles rather than to the priests. The NEB makes this clear with its interpretative translation: "So, summoning the priests, I put the offenders on oath to do as they had promised."

In order to underscore the seriousness of the oath which is administered to the nobles, Nehemiah performs a symbolic action (see similar actions performed by the prophets, e.g., Jer. 13:1-12). He describes his action (v. 13): "I also shook out my lap [NEB fold of my robe] and said, 'So may God shake out every man from his house and from his labor who does not perform this promise.' " Nehemiah's action and plea is a simple but sobering one. May those who go back on their pledge, he says, become like those they have abused; may they know firsthand what it is like to be poor and powerless!

"And All the Assembly Said 'Amen' " (5:13)

This statement is clear—but not as clear as it seems to be. The word "all" does not always signify "everyone." Often it means "many" (e.g., Matt. 8:34). Here the word "all" probably means "majority." Surely, the voice vote of the assembly did not represent the view of some of the wealthy members of the community. No doubt, some of the landowners in the community went along with Nehemiah's plea, but one suspects that they did not do so out of a generous heart. Community pressure as well as pressure from Nehemiah, the Persian administrator (v. 14), must have played a role. If the nobles and officials praised Yahweh and said "Amen," it may have been only with the movement of the lips. Those who have had some experience with leadership in religious institutions know that difficult decisions relating to surrendering of power and money are seldom pleasing to everyone! Public "moral" pressure sometimes brings about a right decision. Although this kind of pressure cannot make people moral, such pressure has a proper place, for it checks irresponsible people in society from bringing other people to ruin. At any rate, whether fully pleased or not, "the people [i.e., the nobles] did as they had promised" (v. 13).

NEHEMIAH: TORAH IN THE HEART (5:14-19)

Correcting a Misuse of Power

For the first time we learn that Nehemiah held the title of "governor" (v. 14) during his stay in Jerusalem (445-433 B.C.E.). The words that follow, in which Nehemiah characterizes his work and rule among the Jews, reveals some kinship to Paul's defense of his ministry in Corinth (e.g., 1 Cor. 4:8-13; 9:3-18). Nehemiah presents himself as a humane person. Neither he nor his "brethren" (probably officials assisting him) burdened the people with a food allowance, which was the prerogative of the Persian governor (v. 14). Even though his position as governor demanded that he feed and entertain many official visitors (vv. 17-18), he did not ask the people to contribute for this expense. Earlier governors were not so considerate (v. 15). By "former governors," Nehemiah was, no doubt, referring to those governors who ruled since the time of Sheshbazzar and Zerubbabel. These rulers, concerning whom we have no information, placed "heavy burdens" on the community (and so reflected Egyptian treatment of the Israelites!; cf. Exod. 1:11, where a different Hebrew term is used). Their arrogant manner was imitated by their servants (vv. 15-16).

"Because of the Fear of God" (5:15)

Nehemiah represented a different kind of rule. The teaching of the covenant — the Torah — was written upon his heart. *He did not claim his rights.* He and his servants worked on the wall; he sought no land for himself (v. 16); and when he saw that the people were bearing heavy burdens, he refused to add to them by demanding the "food allowance" to which he was entitled (vv. 14, 18). Further, Nehemiah declares that he was considerate of the people "because of the fear of God" (v. 15). One should not interpret this statement to mean that Nehemiah acted as he did because he was afraid of God. No! When he attributed his good deeds to the "fear of God," he meant simply that he performed these deeds because he was a pious man who lived his life in accordance with covenant teaching (i.e., Torah). Frequently, the book of Deuteronomy calls upon Israelites to "fear" and to "love" God (e.g., Deut. 6:1-4). "Fear" and "love" in the Bible often have approximately the same meaning, that is, "loyalty" to God and his teaching. For comment on v. 19 see our discussion on 13:31.

SUCCESS IN SIGHT BUT STILL OPPOSITION
Nehemiah 6:1-19

A SOFT VOICE, FOLLOWED BY A THREAT (6:1-9)

Following a summary of the socio-economical-ethical problems that existed in the Jewish community (ch. 5), Nehemiah speaks again of the opposition of outside enemies (ch. 6). The quick success of Nehemiah and his workers in rebuilding the wall surprised his opponents — and strengthened their opposition. Sanballat and Tobiah had ridiculed the efforts of the Jews earlier (4:1-3), but now the wall was nearly finished (v. 1), and they were impressed by what had been done (6:15-16). What the enemies of the Jews thought could not be done was now completed. The Jews under Nehemiah's leadership worked in difficult circumstances, but once committed to this work, they "put their hands to the plow" and did not look back (cf. Luke 9:62). They did not let their enemies intimidate them. Now, success stands before them, but so do their enemies.

Nehemiah Rejects an Invitation for Discussion (6:2-4)

Sanballat and Geshem approach Nehemiah and indicate that they want to talk things over with him (v. 2). Nehemiah is suspicious. The "plains of Ono" (v. 2), where they wish to meet him, is some distance from the protection of friends in Jerusalem, and therefore Nehemiah, no doubt, feels insecure. Believing they wish to harm him — that their request is only a show of friendliness — Nehemiah refuses their invitation to meet. In fact, he refuses four invitations. The reason given for his refusal must have irritated Sanballat and Geshem. Nehemiah declares that he is too busy building the wall (which Sanballat and Geshem want to halt!) to enter into discussion (vv. 3-4). Finally, these two opponents drop the pretext of friendliness. They send by messenger an "open letter" (v. 5) in which they accuse him of traitorous activity. That is, they charge him with planning a revolt against Persia and installing himself as king.

The Accusation: Nehemiah Wants to Be King (6:5-7)

Sanballat and Geshem indicate that they will report their accusation to the Persian king. Earlier, this same charge of rebellion had halted work on the wall (see Ezra 4:11-24). Sanballat and Geshem hope that their threat to inform the Persian king of their suspicions will panic Nehemiah and make him more willing to compromise (as have some of the Jewish nobles; cf. 6:17-19). But Nehemiah is unwavering; he will not be intimidated from doing what he believes to be God's will. His courageous commitment to the creation of a strong Jerusalem is reflected in a later verse of this chapter. The last sentence of v. 9 is translated in the following manner by the RSV: "But now, O God, strengthen thou my hands." However, "O God" is not in the MT. The NEB prefers the LXX reading: "So I applied myself to it with greater energy." Although we believe the RSV to be the better translation, both depict a determined leader who has no plans to give up.

Do "Enemies" Sometimes Have a Point?

From this distance in time, it is very difficult to understand the actual situation. Were Sanballat and Geshem creating these accusations of rebellion out of thin air? Although Nehemiah may not have had rebellion in mind, the past history of the Jews was not fully supportive of his protestations of innocence. Observe also that, according to the accusation, there were "prophets" in the land proclaiming "There is a king in Judah" (v. 7). It is not unlikely that some of Nehemiah's supporters had such hopes for him. From Nehemiah's words we have a "black-and-white" portrayal of the situation. In an earlier discussion (see our comments on Ezra 4), we observed that there was division in the Jewish community concerning the rebuilding of the temple. No doubt there was a similar disagreement concerning the rebuilding of the wall. Surely some Jews saw this activity as a dangerous and unhealthy separatism — even as today in Israel there is disagreement about the defensive-offensive posture of the Israeli government with regard to the Arabs.

Did Nehemiah Misunderstand Tobiah? (6:17-19)

Were the nobles, in part at least, right when they spoke to Nehemiah concerning the good deeds of Tobiah (vv. 17-19)? Is it possible that he was not as bad as Nehemiah thought? Perhaps he had some right on his side? Did he and others oppose the rebuilding of the wall for good reasons? Often we are tempted to depict our opponents as completely evil. But that is seldom the case. Although it is true that the nobles had reasons to speak well of Tobiah (because of business dealings and family relationships), it is also true that in some ways they knew him best. Did they understand correctly Tobiah's fears about a strong Jerusalem?

Actually, the nobles are not too different from Nehemiah. They show friendliness toward Tobiah, but it is also true that Nehemiah's service in the Persian court revealed a friendly understanding of the Persian king and government (Neh. 2:1-8); some people, in fact, must have thought that he had been too friendly to these foreigners. Nehemiah would probably defend his actions by saying that such an approach is simply using common sense. The nobles would no doubt offer the same defense for their relationship to Tobiah.

Nevertheless, it is also true that the preservation of a community depends (sometimes) on one who stands firm and says no when others are saying yes or maybe. Whether an action or a stance is right or wrong often has to do with the time, place, and character of the situation. *There is a time for flexibility and a time for firmness; wisdom is knowing when to prefer the one to the other.*

Did Nehemiah Want to Be King? (6:6-9)

A further complication in the conflict between Nehemiah and his three opponents relates to the identity of Nehemiah himself. He is accused of planning to become king over the restored community (vv. 6-7). Is this a wild charge or does it have some substance? At an earlier time, Zerubbabel, a descendant of David, was enthusiastically presented as a soon-to-be ruler over the Jewish community. If Nehemiah himself was a descendant of David, we could imagine that similar thoughts would be held concerning him also. The accusation that he wanted to be king is easily understood if he comes from the royal family. Even if *he* had no aspirations for kingship, many of his followers, no doubt, would have wanted to cast him in that role (see v. 7 and the reference to prophets proclaiming his kingship).

But does Nehemiah come from the family of David? Ulrich Kellermann (*Nehemia,* 156-59) thinks that Neh. 2:3, 5 point in this direction. Nehemiah's ancestors are buried in the city (i.e., Jerusalem), a place where only royalty are buried. In addition, in v. 5 the Hebrew reads: "the house of the graves of my fathers." This could be a reference to a royal tomb. Further, the fact that

Nehemiah served in the court of the king of Persia (and later was appointed governor over the Jews) may indicate that he was of royal birth. One might ask, if he were a descendant of David, why was his royal character not mentioned? In reply it may be said that after the Zerubbabel debacle, one can understand why the author of the book of Nehemiah would be reticent to underscore Nehemiah's descent from David (note that the author refrains also from reminding the reader of Zerubbabel's Davidic origins). The question of Nehemiah's identity remains a tantalizing one. His family line may have gone back to David, but the evidence is not firm. In any case, if Nehemiah were from the Davidic line, he was a credit to the best of the prophetic hopes concerning the Davidic king. He gave himself to the establishing of Jerusalem, was humble, promoted Torah in the life of the people, established justice, and was compassionate to the poor (cf. Isa. 9:6-7 and 11:1-5).

SHEMAIAH: A FALSE PROPHET (6:10-14)

Nehemiah is a courageous leader, but even the brave sometimes need counsel and encouragement. Whether the two met at the initiative of Shemaiah or of Nehemiah we do not know. Such a meeting between a prophet and government leader was not unusual; earlier prophets had from time to time met with Israelite rulers (e.g., Jer. 38:14-28). Shemaiah is "shut up" in his house (v. 10; cf. Jer. 36:5). We are given no information concerning the reason for this restriction. It does not, however, keep Nehemiah from meeting with him.

Misplaced Trust

Nehemiah went to Shemaiah, believing him to be an authentic prophet. But when he heard the counsel of the man of God, it became evident to him that this servant of God had sold out — he had become the servant of Sanballat and Tobiah. In return for money he was willing to use his calling to undermine Nehemiah and his work. Shemaiah was not the only one who attempted to undermine Nehemiah; other prophets were involved. This group, to whom money was the inspiration for prophecy, included a prophetess, Noadiah.

All people, whether male or female, black or white, Jew or Christian, are capable of this kind of deception. The literature of the world is full of stories about a "trusted" person who turns out to be a deceiver and betrayer. Jacob, Shemaiah, and Judas are the names of three who have broken trust, but the circle is not limited to these alone. The deed of Shemaiah is an act from the past, but the lure to betray the sacred is a continuing one. "Is it I?" the disciples ask; they felt the power of the temptation that caused Judas to fall.

Resisting Panic

Shemaiah urged Nehemiah to flee with him to the temple for safety because some men, he said, wanted to kill him. Nehemiah sees through this advice and realizes that the prophet had said this to panic him into running for safety to the temple. If he, the Persian governor (!) had done so, he would have shown weakness and would have lost standing in the community (v. 11). Our understanding of this situation assumes the alternative reading in the RSV mg of v. 11: "And what man such as I would go into the temple to save his life?" The "sin" that is spoken of in v. 13 does not refer to Nehemiah's entrance into the temple (as if that would have been a sin in a time of emergency); it refers to the lack of faith in God (i.e., if Nehemiah had acted out of fear, he would have sinned).

Nehemiah knows that Shemaiah is an ally of his persistent opponents; therefore he calls out: "Remember Tobiah and San-ballat" (v. 14). In our comments on ch. 4 we have already discussed the matter of vengeance. Nehemiah, obviously, has thoughts of his own and is honest enough to express this anger. But he expresses it in terms of a wish for God's action. His prayer is fervent, but, as in Rom. 12:19, he leaves it to God to repay.

THE WORK ON THE WALL IS FINISHED (6:15-19)

After fifty-two days of hard work, the wall is completed. This appears to be a rather brief period to accomplish such a task, but we do not know how much of the wall had to be rebuilt, nor do we know how completely the wall was restored. In any case, those who watched the Jews work—and who made snide comments about their accomplishment (Neh. 4:1-3)—were surprised when the wall was finished. Although any translation of v. 16 is tenuous, the general sense of the verse is clear: The foreigners were quite amazed, and they recognized that the work on the wall was done with divine help. One is reminded of the "reported" response of the nations as they observed the Israelites' successful flight from Egypt (see Exod. 15:13-16; cf. Mark 15:39).

THESE ARE THE PIONEERS
Nehemiah 7:1-73a

APPOINTMENT OF LEADERS (7:1-2)

Although there are some translation problems in this section (esp. v. 3), the general sense of these verses is not in doubt. The city walls are completed, but these walls provide security only if the people within are cautious and watchful. Gatekeepers, together with "singers and Levites" (cf. 13:22), are appointed to guard the gates.

Further, Nehemiah appoints to leadership under him his own brother, Hanani, and the respected Hananiah, who was "a more faithful and God-fearing man than many" (v. 2). Together, these three leaders work to make Jerusalem safe and, once again, great.

SECURITY ALERT (7:3-4)

Additional precautions are taken to strengthen the security of the city. Citizen guards are appointed to keep watch for danger. Although Jerusalem's enemies may have been impressed with the quick repair of the walls (Neh. 6:16), Nehemiah believed that they still intended harm to the city and its citizens. The city was very vulnerable to attack because it was not fully settled (v. 4; cf. 11:1-2).

THE BOOK OF GENEALOGY (7:5)

Quite likely, the sparse population within the city is the reason for the decision to have the people "enrolled by genealogy" (v. 5). With this information one could plan for the growth of the population of the city, that is, it would be possible to settle people of various clans within the city. As one can see from Neh. 11:1-2, Jerusalem citizenship was not exactly prized by many Jews. According to this passage, lots were cast in order to determine which

120

people were to live in Jerusalem; those who abided by the decision of the lot (or perhaps volunteered on their own) to live in Jerusalem were "blessed" by their countrymen. No doubt, the hardship and danger associated with Jerusalem caused people to settle elsewhere.

The intention of v. 5 is to discover the various clans represented and to ask each clan to take its responsibility in settling the capital city. No one clan or family should have to bear the hardship of life in Jerusalem.

Nehemiah indicates that he found "the book of genealogy," which turns out to be basically the same list as the one recorded in Ezra 2. However, we do not know whether this census was ever used as a guide to settle Jerusalem. We hear no more about it. The only plan for the increasing of the population of Jerusalem (that we know about) is the one mentioned in Neh. 11:1-2, and this plan has to do with casting lots, not with establishing genealogy.

For vv. 6-72, see our comments on Ezra 2.

EZRA READS THE TORAH
Nehemiah 7:73b – 8:18

CHRONOLOGICAL PROBLEMS

Nehemiah's narrative, which has centered on the difficulties the Jews had in rebuilding the walls around Jerusalem, is broken off at this point; it resumes again in ch. 11. Many interpreters are convinced that chs. 8 – 9 relate to the activity of Ezra alone. Some scholars would place these chapters immediately following Ezra 10 (see also 1 Esd. 9:37-55, which includes the material in Neh. 8:1-13 after Ezra 10); others would insert them following Ezra 8. No fully satisfying explanation for this disruption has been offered, although the suggestion by Richard Coggins (*Ezra and Nehemiah*, 107) has merit: the editor of the Ezra-Nehemiah material (whom Coggins believes to be the Chronicler) had his own idea about chronology: "For him the maxim, 'first things first' meant, not as it might for us, a chronological order, but an order of importance. The temple must come first, then the purifying of the community [discussed in the book of Ezra], then the building of the outer walls of the city, and so finally all could reach a grand climax in the reading of the law. Neh. 8 – 9 could be regarded as the conclusion of the work of restoration, to which the additional material in Neh. 10 – 13 was merely a supplement."

THE PEOPLE WANT TO HEAR TORAH (7:73b – 8:8)

The "seventh month" in ancient Israel was a festival month in which the Day of Atonement and the Feast of Booths were observed (cf. Lev. 23:27, 34). Also, the first day of that month may have been celebrated as a New Year's day (Lev. 23:24). Our text mentions only the "seventh month" (7:73); we are given no information concerning the year. Some interpreters think that this event is to be connected to the narrative in Ezra 7, which speaks of Ezra coming to Jerusalem in the "fifth month" of the seventh year of Artaxerxes (Ezra 7:7-8). Two months later (in the "seventh month"), it is argued, occurs this event described in Neh. 8. This is possible, but it seems clear, as Ryle has noted (*Ezra and Nehemiah,* 237), that the compiler of Nehemiah wanted to portray the events of ch. 8 as happening after the completion of the wall, which took place on "the twenty-fifth day of the month Elul," which is the sixth month (Neh. 6:15).

A Torah-True People

Whoever set this material down in this place wanted to depict the Jews as a faithful people who sought to live according to Torah. As is clear from the rebukes of both Ezra and Nehemiah, some people in the restored community rebelled against the old traditions and teachings, but many people wanted to be Torah-true and thus supported the work of Ezra and Nehemiah. In the midst of the cultic observances of the seventh month, which reminds the community of Yahweh's saving activity in early Israel, these people *ask* to hear "the book of the law of Moses which the LORD had given to Israel" (8:1). At the beginning of a new era in the history of Israel, the returned Jews demonstrate their desire to listen to the Torah, which holds out success and life to those who obey its commandments (cf., e.g., Josh. 1:7 and Deut. 30:15-30).

Gathering for Worship (8:1-6)

The character of this meeting is a bit difficult to ascertain; it appears to reflect an established cultic (worship) pattern. Observe, for example, the gathering of the people (the congregation) into the square (8:1); the request to hear the Torah (8:1); the pulpit (Heb. *migdal-'ets,* lit. "tower of wood," 8:4); the opening of the "book" to which the people responded by standing (8:5); the blessing and the congregational response, which involved saying "Amen," raising the hands, and bowing the head in worship; the reading of the Torah by Ezra (8:3) and by the Levites (8:7-8). As many have noted, this pattern of worship is reflected in later synagogue practice.

Worship outside the Temple (8:1)

This large gathering of people takes place in a large square in the city—not in the temple. Possibly the meeting took place in an area before the temple (cf. Ezra 10:1). Although the temple and its ritual were considered to be of great importance for the community, significant worship could take place outside the temple's confines. Yahweh's teaching (i.e., the Torah), like Yahweh,

123

was not limited to the temple building. The temple with its ritual was made for the sake of Torah, not Torah for the sake of the temple. The temple is important, but more important is Torah and obedience to it. This is the firm declaration of the eighth- and seventh-century prophets.

This gathering of Jews for "worship" in the temple square should not be overemphasized, because there must have been other times when some form of worship took place outside the holy building. But the fact that such a service could occur apart from the temple and its symbolism illustrates that Israel did not absolutely need the temple in order to approach God. This fact helps to explain Israel's difficult movement from a temple religion to a synagogue faith which centered on the study of and obedience to Torah. Judaism does not despise holy places, but its emphasis on Torah enables it to escape "imprisonment" in sanctuaries. Jesus' teaching concerning sacrifice and the temple affirms this same basic truth (see, e.g., Matt. 12:1-8).

The Levites Interpret the Torah Reading (8:7-8)

It is difficult to define exactly the participation of the Levites because of the ambiguity of the Hebrew term (from *parash*) which the RSV renders "clearly." The basic meaning of this root is "to separate." Some scholars believe that this meaning points to the idea of "translation"; others think that "interpretation" is what the root *parash* demands. If "translation" is the correct rendering here (into Aramaic?; cf. Neh. 13:24), it supports an ancient Jewish tradition which places the origin of the Aramaic Targums (in their oral form) during the activity of Ezra (B.T. *Megillah* 3a).

Whatever the exact rendering of this word, the sense of the verse is clear; it has to do with interpretation (which, of course, would involve translation). The Levites read from the Torah, "and they gave the sense, so that the people understood the reading" (v. 8; cf. v. 7). The "book of the law of Moses" (v. 1; cf. v. 8) from which both Ezra and the Levites read was probably some form of the Pentateuch. We should not imagine that the complete Pentateuch was read at this time. Verse 3 states that Ezra read "from it" (lit. "in it"), that is, he read selections from this book of the law.

A HOLY DAY, A DAY OF JOY (8:9-12)

The People Weep When the Torah Is Read (8:9)

As the Torah selections are read to the assembly, the people begin to weep. Why? Usually both Jewish and Christian commentators assume that the people wept because the reading of the Torah reminded them of their sins and those of their fathers (cf. 2 Chron. 34:19-21). This interpretation claims support from v. 10, "do not be grieved" (from Heb. ʿ*atsab*). However, the text itself does not mention sin as the reason for this response of the people. Yehezkel Kaufmann gives an alternative explanation that deserves consideration (*History of the Religion of Israel,* 4:379). He believes that it was an emotional response to the reading of the Torah: "The narrative indicates clearly that Ezra's intention was not to cause weeping. Ezra wanted the day to be one of rejoicing of the Law. The tears expressed, it seems, a deep mass emotion which might break out both in weeping and rejoicing. The assemblage heard and understood things they had not known, statutes which had not been observed, unwonted explanations of the word of God. Emotions rose to the point of tears."

For Torah: Eat, Drink, and Rejoice (8:10-12)

The proper response to the reading of the Law on this joyous day (cf. Lev. 23:24) is not weeping but rejoicing, declares Ezra ("Nehemiah" is probably a later addition to the text; see D. J. A. Clines, *Ezra, Nehemiah, Esther,* 185). He urges the people on this holy day, this day of happiness, to "eat the fat and drink sweet wine." This is the way that one should celebrate Torah, because the Torah, like food, revives life (cf. Ps. 19:7 together with Lam. 1:11, 19); further, drinking "sweet wine" is most appropriate because the Torah itself is very sweet (cf. Ps. 19:10 with Neh. 8:10; in both places Heb. *mathaq* is used). It is fitting that the people "make great rejoicing" because the Torah brings "rejoicing" to the heart (cf. Neh. 8:12 and Ps. 19:8; Heb. *samah* occurs in both passages). In Neh. 9:13, Yahweh is celebrated as the one who has given Israel "right ordinances and true laws, good statutes and commandments." The Torah has not been "forced" upon Israel; it is a gift by one who wants fullness of life for humankind.

The Torah Creates Shalom

The Torah comes from the heart of Israel's saving, holy God. It does not oppress; it does not set lines of strain on the face or heaviness in the heart. It deserves the title given to it in the Jewish tradition: "the Torah of life." The fall festival of *Simhat Torah* (Rejoicing in the Law) emphasizes how highly treasured the Law is in the Jewish community. Without Torah, life would be chaotic (cf. Jer. 5:1-5; Hab. 1:3-4; see also Hos. 4:1-3). The Torah builds true community; obedience to its teachings make it possible for everyone (not just the rich and powerful) to enjoy life. Because the Torah creates *shalom* for the community and the individual, people "love" and "delight in" the Law (Ps. 119:97, 70). When they are far removed from Israel they look longingly for its light on their life (Isa. 42:4). In the past, some Christian theologians and preachers have set the Law over against Jesus, but this is to misrepresent the Law that was known to the psalmists, prophets, and later leaders of the Jewish community. It is significant for the understanding both of the Law and of Jesus to observe that the NT describes Jesus and his teaching in terms that remind one of Torah (John 4:14 [bread]; 6:35 [water]; 14:6 ["the way, and the truth, and the life"]). Rabbinic and modern Jewish worship literature speak of the law in terms of oil, water, food, and life.

"The Joy of the LORD Is Your Strength" (8:10)

Israel owes her life to Yahweh. Especially in the Exodus, Yahweh opened up to Israel a new way of living; he offered a future to Israel. The song of praise sung by "Moses and the people" after escaping from the Egyptians (Exod. 15) describes eloquently this marvelous event as well as Israel's joyous response to Yahweh's saving act. The Exodus was not the last act which Yahweh performed on behalf of Israel; it was the beginning of a relationship in which Yahweh continues to seek life and future for Israel. Rejoicing in the God who brought them out of the "iron furnace" (Deut. 4:20) reminds them of the hope they have in the most distressing situations. Further, remembering Yahweh and rejoicing in him gives Israel strength to say yes to his way of life and no to those paths that lead to oppression and ruin.

True Celebration Means Sharing

The celebration described in 8:10-12 is a rejoicing in Yahweh that also reflects his character — his teaching. The people who celebrate before Yahweh with eating and drinking share food and drink with those who do not have such provisions. Most likely they do not have these provisions because they are poor (so indicates the LXX, which the NEB apparently followed; cf. Deut. 14:29; 16:10-12; 26:12-13; Esth. 9:22). The act of sharing recorded here is a "ritual" act that reminds us of the kind of generosity we are to *express in everyday life* (see, e.g., Nehemiah's example, Neh. 5:14-18). "Generosity" which exists only as a part of religious ritual is nothing but a clanging *"symbol"* (in the spirit, if not the letter, of 1 Cor. 13:1).

THE LAW: OBSERVE THE FEAST OF BOOTHS (8:13-18)

On the second day of the seventh month, the leaders of the community met to study the Law with Ezra. In accordance with the commands of God to Moses (Lev. 23:33-43; Deut. 16:13-17), they make preparations to observe the Feast of Booths. It is a week-long festival beginning on the fifteenth day of the month. This celebration, which was observed in the autumn, took on the characteristics of a harvest festival (Deut. 16:13-15), but in Lev. 23:42-43 it is associated with the Exodus. As the returned exiles celebrated the Feast of Booths and remembered the Exodus from Egypt, they would have reason to thank God that his saving acts did not come to an end in the time of Moses, because without his intervention they would not have been able to return to the land from their captivity. He has performed mighty acts of deliverance in the past, but he is not a God of the past. Today Jews, especially, remember the Exodus, and Christians remember the Resurrection, but not simply because they are past events. Jews and Christians remember these events because these "past" events have broken out of the past and have become "present" to each generation.

The Feast of Booths, which was celebrated during the time of Joshua (v. 17), must have retained strong memory of the Exodus. This same emphasis must have been present as the returned exiles under the leadership of Ezra observed the festival by dwelling in booths which they themselves had made. It was a memory that would excite a "very great rejoicing" (v. 17). The "man of war" (Exod. 15:3), the one who "redeemed" and "purchased" his people (Exod. 15:13, 16) and established his "sanctuary" in the land (Exod. 15:17) — this one still lives in the Jewish community.

No Celebration Like This One (8:17)

Verse 17 declares (with reference to observing the Feast of Booths) that "from the days of Jeshua [i.e., Joshua] the son of Nun to that day the people of Israel had not done so." This statement is difficult to understand because evidence indicates that this feast was celebrated after the time of Joshua and before the time of Ezra (see, e.g., 2 Chron. 7:8ff. and Ezra 3:4). It is possible that our passage is simply an example of hyperbole (cf. 2 Chron. 30:26; 35:18) that intends to underline the wholehearted character of the celebration. However, Kaufmann proposes an alternative explanation (*History of the Religion of Israel*, 4:380-82). He observes that the celebration of the Feast of Booths described in

Lev. 23:33-43 does not agree fully with that set forth in Deut. 16:13-17 and 31:10-11. Further, he notices that the description of the observance of the feast in Neh. 8 owes something to Lev. 23:33-43 (e.g., living in the booths) and to Deut. 16:16-17 (e.g., the celebration focuses at one "place"; in Neh. 8:15-16 that "place" is Jerusalem). In addition, the celebration of Neh. 8 differs to some degree from Lev. 23 and from Deut. 16 (e.g., the trees named in Neh. 8 are not the same ones mentioned in Lev. 23, and Deut. 16 does not mention any special branches at all).

It appears that *this* observance of the Feast of Booths represented a departure from the traditions by which Israel had earlier celebrated this festival (cf. also the comments of Ryle, *Ezra and Nehemiah*, 247); therefore one would be correct to say that the feast had never been observed quite *in this manner*. But, though the form of celebration changed, the God remembered and praised in this festival is the saving God known in Joshua's time.

REPENTANCE AND CONFESSION
Nehemiah 9:1-37

SOLEMN WORSHIP (9:1-5)

From Feasting to Fasting (9:1)

The dating of this chapter presents many difficulties. For good reasons, many interpreters believe that originally this material had another context. For example, it is pointed out that vv. 36-37 would hardly have been written concerning Persian rule because this rule was not oppressive. However, there is little agreement among scholars as to its actual date or context. We also recognize the difficulties that this chapter presents, but are convinced that the editor of Nehemiah wanted future readers to see the events of this chapter as following upon those narrated in ch. 8 (see, e.g., the reference to "the twenty-fourth day of this month" in 9:1 and the mention of Nehemiah in 10:1). The LXX underlines the continuity between chs. 8 and 9 by adding the words "and Ezra said" (see RSV) in 9:6. Our comments on these verses will, therefore, assume the context (the only context we know for certain!) that the editor has given us.

Separation for the Right Reason (9:2)

Other passages in Ezra and Nehemiah insist on the separation of Jews from other peoples in order to protect the Jewish community from pollution (see, e.g., Ezra 10:11 and Neh. 13:23-31). Although, as we have mentioned, this concern was a real one, insistence on separation for this reason (esp. in our democratic world) seems harsh and narrow-minded. Perhaps we can understand this "negative" reason for separation better if we keep in mind the present passage, which underlines the fact that "separation" has nothing to do with simply disliking someone. Separation has to do, principally, with religious commitment — with the idea of covenant. One who did not own Yahweh as king and

129

his teachings as Law was an alien and ruinous force within the close-knit Jewish community.

As v. 2 suggests, however, this idea of covenant has another aspect: *Only those who were in covenant with Yahweh were responsible when this covenant was broken.* Foreigners who had not taken an oath to be servants of Yahweh were not bound by the covenant. They had not promised to obey Yahweh's teachings; therefore they could hardly be expected to confess that they had disobeyed them. The Jews, however, *were* in covenant with Yahweh, and therefore they considered themselves as responsible for their sins. It is this kind of reasoning that explains the action recorded in v. 2: "And the Israelites separated themselves from all foreigners, and stood and confessed their sins and the iniquities of their fathers."

We Have Sinned

It would have been easy for Israel to blame all of her difficulties on other people (and certainly many hardships came Israel's way because of foreign rulers), but she did not play the game called "It's all someone else's fault." This chapter is an impressive testimony to Israel's ability (under sensitive leadership) to be self-critical, to recognize her own sins. She was not easy on herself (see, e.g., 9:16-17, 26, 29; cf. the prayer of Ezra in Ezra 9:6-7).

Unfortunately, some Christians (including influential Church Fathers) have misinterpreted Israel's confessions of sins. Instead of viewing these confessions as a witness to Israel's deep desire to be loyal to Yahweh and his teachings, they have interpreted them to mean that Israel is an especially sinful people and therefore deserving of all the suffering that has come upon her. This perverse and unchristian interpretation has fueled a centuries-long anti-Semitism. It refuses to recognize that Israel's sins are not different in kind from the sins practiced within the Christian community; it will not acknowledge that in Christian, as well as Jewish, tradition, we are called upon to confess our sins and repent of them. It is those who do not — who will not — confess their sins who are really the "wicked" ones (cf. 1 John 1:8-10).

The Church and the Confession of Sin

Missing in the NT are these kinds of corporate confessions of sin. The absence of such confessions from this part of the canon that the Church most often uses may explain why corporate confessions of sin, which focus specifically on wrongs the Church has committed, are not prominent in some Christian denominations. However, the Church must take the risk, as Israel did, and confess the sins that have occurred in her own history. It is a risk to do this, because people will then know from our own words that we also are a sinful people. In doing so, however, we become responsible to the covenant which we have with God through Jesus Christ. Further, by means of sincere confession, we demonstrate our own sensitivity to the voice of God. A church which continues to call secular institutions and individuals to confession and repentance must learn to confess and repent itself.

ABRAHAM IS FAITHFUL (9:6-8)

Abraham "Believed" and Was "Faithful"

The God who created the world (v. 6) chose Abraham (v. 7)! In this choice Yahweh was not disappointed because he found him "faithful" (v. 8). The Hebrew root is *'aman,* a term also used in Gen. 15:6: "And he [i.e., Abraham] believed [Heb. *'aman*] the LORD; and he reckoned it to him as righteousness." Christians have often set "believed" (understood as "having faith") in this verse over against "faithful" (understood as "doing works"). They have done so under the influence of an exaggerated Pauline theology. Paul refers to Gen. 15:6 several times in his epistles (Rom. 4:3, 9, 22-23; Gal. 5:6), and these passages, at first glance, appear to support a distinction between "believing" and "being faithful." But Paul knows that belief which does not have the substance of faithfulness is nothing (Gal. 5:16-24). Perhaps Paul's enthusiasm over the marvelous grace of God revealed in Christ sometimes led him to make hyperbolic statements that obscured his more careful and basic position. In any case, James makes clear (what I think is implicit in Paul's writings) that "belief" or "faith" must include "faithfulness" if it is to be pleasing to God (Jas. 2:14-26).

Abraham: Justified by Faith — by Works

What a surprise! After Paul had used Abraham as an illustration of one who was "justified by faith" (Gal. 3:6-9), James holds up this same patriarch as an example of one who was "justified by works" (Jas. 2:21; contrast Rom. 4:2!). Further, "faith was active along with his works, and faith was completed by works, and the scripture was fulfilled which says, 'Abraham believed God, and it was reckoned to him as righteousness' " (Jas. 2:22-23). In Neh. 9:8, the Hebrew root *'aman* is correctly translated "faithful." One could also render it "loyal." Nehemiah 9:8 stands as an early Jewish interpretation of Gen. 15:6; it reflects an understanding of faith that has influenced the comments recorded in Jas. 2:21-24.

131

In addition, this passage asserts that Yahweh is faithful, that is, he keeps his promises ("thou hast fulfilled thy promise"; cf. Gen. 12:1-2 and 17:1-8; see also Neh. 9:23-25). The declaration "thou art righteous" (v. 8) probably also has the sense of being faithful, that is, God has done the right thing — he has kept his word.

The Children of Abraham?

In Neh. 9:8, Abraham the faithful man (the true man of faith) stands as the example of what God wants of Israel. But, unfortunately, not all the children of "father" Abraham were really his children (cf. Gal. 3:7). Rather than follow in the footsteps of faithful Abraham, "they stiffened their neck" (Neh. 9:16-17), "committed great blasphemies" (vv. 18, 26), "were disobedient and rebelled against" Yahweh, cast aside the Law, and killed the prophets (v. 26; cf. Matt. 23:37). They rejected the way of Abraham and took on the ways of the Egyptians! As Pharaoh "acted insolently" (v. 10; Hebrew root *zid*) toward the Hebrews in Egypt, so the Israelites "acted presumptuously" (vv. 16 and 29; the same Hebrew root, *zid*) toward the commandments of Yahweh. The way of life we abhor in others is frequently not very far removed from our own hearts.

The sneering question of Pharaoh at the time of the Exodus ("Who is Yahweh?"; cf. Exod. 5:2) and his continued refusal to obey Yahweh is reflected in the Israelite community by those who cast aside the Law (v. 26) and do what they want to do. The cry of the Law and the Prophets against oppression has as its background the temptation of the Israelites to oppress each other as the Egyptians once oppressed the Hebrews. Both Synagogue and Church face the same temptation today, that is, they believe in God but are tempted to live as those who are alien to the community of faith (see, e.g., Eph. 4:17-24; Matt. 6:7).

YAHWEH, THE GENEROUS GIVER (9:9-31)

This section represents a continuing theme in the OT. It might be titled: "Israel's rebellious behavior in response to the gracious acts of God." This text, and others like it in the OT, are *not* saying that the Israelites are the worst of people. The truth is that they were no worse than other people in the ancient Near East, and, with regard to morality, they were better than most. But Israel is not judged by how she compares to other peoples; she is judged by how she relates to Yahweh, her covenant partner. Out of love for Israel (a love unexplainable and unmerited) Yahweh bound himself in a covenant with Israel, and in this relationship he proved to be loyal, loving, and generous. Nehemiah 9 emphasizes this generosity of Yahweh. It speaks, as do few other chapters in the Bible, of what *Yahweh has given* to Israel. The verb "to give" *(nathan)* occurs fourteen times in this chapter, including the second occurrence of *nathan* in 9:8 which is not translated in the LXX or in the RSV. In 9:10 *nathan* is translated by "perform" and in 9:35 by "set." Yahweh *gave:*

Land (vv. 8, 15, 35-36)
"Signs and wonders" (v. 10)
"True laws, good statutes" (v. 13). See comments on 8:9-12.
Food and drink (vv. 15, 20)
His "good Spirit" (v. 20)
Victory over enemies (vv. 22, 24)
Punishment for Israel but also redemption (v. 27)
His "great goodness" (v. 35)

God's Steadfast Love

Yahweh's love for Israel has a "second mile" quality to it. Even though Israel repeatedly broke the covenant relationship, Yahweh considered himself bound to it. He does not give up on wayward Israel; when she falls into need and she cries for help, he comes to her aid (vv. 26-31). Although Israel frequently disappointed Yahweh by her rebelliousness, "nevertheless," it is confessed, "in thy great mercies thou didst not make an end of them or forsake them; for thou art a gracious and merciful God" (v. 31). Here is the wonderful mystery of God: He is for us, even after we have been against him. His ways are higher than our ways (Isa. 55:6-9; Hos. 11:8-9); he does not treat us as we deserve to be treated (Ps. 103:10-11).

ONCE MORE, O YAHWEH, REMEMBER US (9:32-35)

Now and then the Bible alludes to the "good old days," days when Israel lived in a close, faithful relationship to Yahweh (e.g., Jer. 2:2-3). Usually, however, the good part of "the good old days," as Lüthi observes (*Die Bauleute Gottes*, 127), was Yahweh himself; although his people were often faithless, he remained faithful and compassionate (cf. 2 Tim. 2:13). If Yahweh should "mark iniquities, . . . who could stand" (Ps. 130:3)? No one. But Yahweh is compassionate; he forgives (Ps. 130:4, 7-8). It is this abundant mercy of Yahweh that gives Israel hope for the future. The appeal to Yahweh, with which v. 32 begins ("Now therefore"), is not founded on any merit that Israel has; it rests on Yahweh's reputation as the God who continues to keep "covenant and steadfast love" (cf. Dan. 9:18), even though the covenant has been broken by the faithlessness of Israel.

The Just God (9:33)

The prayer calls upon this gracious God to give thought to the suffering that Israel has experienced from foreign domination — a domination that goes back, at least, to Assyrian rule in the 8th century B.C.E. Once again, the sins of the past and present generations are confessed (vv. 33-35), with the admission that God was "just" *(tsaddiq)* in his punishment of them (v. 33; cf. Dan. 9:14). Israel's continuing rebellion left Yahweh no other option. However, being a "just" God does not refer exclusively to Yahweh's punishing judgment of sinful people. It speaks also of the God who fulfills promises to a faithful servant (Neh. 9:8; RSV has translated *tsaddiq* here by "righteous"). Further, the "just" God is also the merciful one (cf. Ps. 116:5) whose "righteous acts" (Dan. 9:16; *tsedaqah*) encourage sinners to look to him for deliverance (see also Ps. 51:14, where a forgiven sinner sings happily of Yahweh's "deliverance," *tsedaqah*). Yahweh's righteousness goes beyond the strict letter of the covenant teaching; it reaches out to rescue and bring back to himself those who have broken away from his family. As we said above, if God's righteousness were not like this (if, e.g., he should "mark iniquities"; Ps. 130:1), no one would be left to stand before him. This righteousness of God that "reaches out" is the good news announced in the NT: In Jesus Christ the saving righteousness of God is revealed to humankind (Rom. 1:17; 3:21-22). Jews and Christians count on God's righteousness (as did the Jews of Nehemiah's time), because only this righteousness that "goes beyond righteousness" gives us hope for the future.

WE ARE STILL SLAVES (9:36-37)

Free but under Restraint

To be "almost free" is never enough; if you are a slave, "almost free" means that you are still a slave. Under Persian rule the Jews were "almost free." Jews did not despise this "almost free" existence, however, because under benevolent monarchs the Jews were free to return to the land and there to rebuild the temple and the city of Jerusalem. The writings of both Ezra and Nehemiah portray the Persian rulers as cooperative and fair (even generous) toward the Jewish community (cf., e.g., Ezra 1:1-4; 7:21-26; Neh. 2:4-9); without their help it is doubtful that the Jews could have rebuilt the temple (e.g., cf. Ezra 6:14).

"The Law of the Hour"

Recognizing the importance of Persian support in rebuilding the Jewish community in the land, Jews, under the leadership of Ezra and Nehemiah, cooperated with the Persians — apparently even to the point of allowing prayers to be offered for the Persian king and his son (Ezra 6:10). No doubt Ezra and Nehemiah argued for this kind of cooperation on the basis of what Jews later on called "the law of the hour *(hora'ath sha'ah)*." This "law" operated in new or difficult situations where the traditional law did not give full direction. The traditional law (i.e., the Sinai teaching) gave little practical help on how to rebuild a Jewish state when you are a people subject to a larger power. *The "law of the hour" was really the law of common sense.* That is, in order to survive and create a future, one may do acts of which the traditional teaching may not approve — providing these acts do not pervert the core of faith (see, e.g., the discussion of Eliezer Berkovits, *Not in Heaven: The Nature and Function of Halakha,* 67-70).

Living under Persian Rule but Longing for Full Freedom

But "getting along" is not fully satisfying. Every day the Jews are reminded that they are under the rule of Persians. They are, in fact, *still slaves* in the very land which God gave to their fathers so that they might "enjoy its fruit and its good gifts" (vv. 36-37). Even though the Persians proved to be benevolent rulers, Jews could not be happy about their "subject status" (cf. Ezra 9:8-9). This discontent may be seen in the oracles of Haggai and Zechariah, prophets who prophesied earlier in the Persian period. These prophets envisioned Zerubbabel as a Jewish monarch who would release Israel from this (benevolent!) bondage. It is not surprising, therefore, that Jewish leaders in the days of Ezra and Nehemiah were "in great distress" (v. 37). Although there is no direct request that God should intervene in order to deliver the Jews from this "great distress," it appears certain that such a deliverance was the hope of the heart (cf. v. 32: "let not all the hardship seem little to thee that has come upon us").

135

A FIRM COVENANT
Nehemiah 9:38 – 10:39

CHRONOLOGY AGAIN

Many scholars believe that this chapter belonged originally to another time period. Almost every interpreter agrees, however, that the editor who brought the Ezra-Nehemiah material together intended this event of covenant-making to follow ch. 9 (see, e.g., "Because of this" in 9:38, which in the MT is 10:1). The prayer in ch. 9, which rehearses Yahweh's saving deeds, confesses the faithlessness of Israel, and calls upon Yahweh to consider the "great distress" of the Jewish community, forms a believable background to this "firm covenant" described in this chapter. If chs. 9 and 10 were not originally related, the editor who brought them together performed his task with skill.

"A FIRM COVENANT" MEANS: A COVENANT OF FAITHFULNESS (9:38)

One is surprised to find that the customary term for "covenant" (*berith;* cf., e.g., Neh. 9:8; Ezra 10:3) is not used to describe this covenanting act in 9:38. The one Hebrew term employed here, which must be translated by the use of two English words, is *'amanah.* This Hebrew term is translated in various ways (e.g., RSV "firm covenant"; NEB "binding declaration"). It comes from the Hebrew root *'aman,* which means be steady or faithful. This same Hebrew root was used of Abraham in 9:8. It is said of Abraham that God found "his heart *faithful* [a niphal participle of *'aman*] before thee." Although "a firm covenant" is a good translation of the Hebrew term *'amanah* in 9:38, it could also be rendered "a faithful agreement."

Children of Abraham

Nowhere else in the OT does *'amanah* occur as a synonym for *berith* (covenant). Why is it used in this passage? Possibly the

136

reference to Abraham in 9:7-8 has influenced its use here. According to the confession of faith in 9:6ff., the Creator of the world (9:6) chose Abraham for himself. This ancestor of Israel proved to be "faithful" (same basic Hebrew root, *'aman*) to Yahweh; therefore, Yahweh concluded a covenant with him (9:7-8). In this covenant, God promised to give Abraham the land of Canaan, a promise that Yahweh fulfilled (9:8). As Abraham was faithful so also was Yahweh! What follows these verses, which speak of the faithfulness of Abraham, is a story of unfaithfulness — a story that ends in judgment. Among the Jewish exiles, there were those who had ears to hear and eyes to see. They learned from father Abraham that, if they were to have a future, they must be people of faithfulness. Therefore, the people are called to enter a firm or faithful covenant agreement.

The "Firm Covenant" and the "New Covenant"

Yahweh wants his people to be, like Abraham, faithful in the heart (9:8). The hope for a "new covenant" in Jeremiah (*berith hadashah;* Jer. 31:31-34) expresses the same basic thought. According to Jeremiah, Yahweh has long enough endured the solemn phrases which sound impressive but are empty and foreign to the heart. People say very piously, "As the LORD lives" (Jer. 5:2), but their heart is not in it. Jeremiah called them back to the *old* way (i.e., to the way of Torah written on the heart; cf. Deut. 6:4-6; 11:18; 30:11-14), but for the people of Jeremiah's time, it was a *new* way!

Jesus addressed the same kind of falseness when he spoke of people in his day who said easily "Lord, Lord" but whose actions contradicted their words (Matt. 7:21-23). The temptation to be "merely" religious — to adopt a religious posture — is a danger to every age and community. The old way modeled by Abraham and Moses (the way of loyalty in the heart) is all too often a new way for us.

The NT declares that Jesus has brought about a "new covenant," but this covenant is not something that one inherits by merely repeating an "I-believe-in-Christ" formula (i.e., saying "Lord, Lord"). We participate in this covenant when we take it to heart, when we do what he commands us to do. On this basic principle there is full agreement between Jer. 31:31-34, Neh. 9:38, and the teaching of Jesus in Matt. 7:21-23. For further comment, see Fredrick Holmgren, "A New Covenant? For Whom?" *The Ecumenist* 22 (1984): 38-41.

WITH OATHS AND CURSES (10:1-29)

Promising with Signed Names

The leaders of the community sign the covenant document (vv. 1-27) — *because* it was already written on their heart — and the rest of the people join with them in swearing allegiance. The latter group includes other eminent leaders as well as some wayward Jews who, having pulled away from their association with non-Jews ("the peoples of the lands," v. 28), now have returned to the faith of their fathers (see our comments on Ezra 6:21). It is a solemn ceremony, one that involves the taking of oaths and the swearing of curses (v. 29). The people promise "to walk in God's law *[torah]* . . . and to observe and do all the commandments of the LORD our Lord and his ordinances and his statutes" (v. 29).

The commitment is to the whole Torah "given by Moses," but the emphasis is upon commandments, ordinances, and statutes that have special relevance for the situation facing the postexilic community. This procedure *seems* to be foreign to "heart religion" — to the religion that the prophets called for. As we noted above, however, we should probably assume that most of the people who signed the covenant document and swore allegiance to the Torah did so because *the desire to obey was already in the heart.*

It may be noted at this point also that there are dangers in some forms of "heart religion." Jews sometimes speak of "cardiac Judaism." This phrase refers to those whose religion is of a very general type; they have a "Jewish heart" but that is about all; in important areas of life there is little that is substantial about their Judaism. This "cardiac" type of faith afflicts the Christian Church as well.

DIFFICULT DAYS OFTEN CALL FOR
HARD DECISIONS (10:30-39)

True Religion Cannot Be Merely General Principles

One can summarize the obligations of the covenant relationship in general terms (e.g., love and faithfulness), but a covenant relationship that only affirms these general principles and is empty of specific content is meaningless. People live in specific contexts and these contexts call for specific responses. Difficult times, especially those times that threaten the survivial of a community, often make an urgent call for special or specific responses. Verses 30-39 contain that kind of call to the postexilic community. The general themes of love, faithfulness, and reverence are present in this passage; they are reflected in the response of the people to the specific issues referred to in the following paragraphs.

No Marriages with Foreigners

The people promise not to enter into marriages with foreigners, that is, with people who stand outside the covenant. Ezra 10:18 speaks only of marriages of Jewish men to foreign women. Here and in Ezra 9:12 intermarriage is outlawed for both Jewish men and women. See our discussion on the above passages and on Neh. 13:23-29.

The Holiness of the Sabbath Will Be Preserved

The Sabbath and other holy days are reaffirmed. Sabbath *purchases* from non-Jewish merchants are forbidden, even though the Torah does not expressly forbid this action (cf. Exod. 20:10-11; 34:21; 35:3). It is apparent that the Sabbath laws had undergone continuing interpretation. Amos 8:5 assumes a law against *selling* (but not against buying) on the Sabbath. Nehemiah 10:31 reflects a movement toward a more strict observance of the Sabbath (see also Jer. 17:21, which preserves a prohibition against carrying burdens on the Sabbath).

Although the teaching here does not reflect the "words" of Torah concerning Sabbath observance, it does reflect the "spirit" of Torah. The activity of these non-Jewish merchants was destroying the sanctity of the Sabbath ("Remember the sabbath day, to keep it holy"; Exod. 20:8); therefore the "spirit" of Torah, if not the "word" of Torah, forbids buying from these merchants. See the discussion below on Neh. 13:15-22. On the above verses, see the significant article of D. J. A. Clines, "Nehemiah 10 as an Example of Early Jewish Exegesis," *JSOT* 21 (1981): 111-17.

The Poor Will Be Protected

The land is to lie fallow in the seventh year. During this seventh year, when the land is not cultivated or planted, the poor may help themselves to whatever grows on it (Exod. 23:11). Further, debts are to be forgiven every seventh year (cf. Deut. 15:1-5). Although this law must have created an economic problem for the community (i.e., those who lend money are threatened with loss; cf. Deut. 15:9), the intention of the law is to help the poor.

The House of God Will Be Honored (10:32-39)

As we read this section we should remember how prominent Zion, the temple, and temple ritual are in the book of Psalms.

139

Although temples and sanctuaries *could become* places of sin that anger God (cf. Amos 4:4-5; 5:4-5), it *was* in the temple that people were nourished by the "presence" of the God who chose them for himself. The customs and ritual described in these verses clearly come from another time and place in history, but the piety that was native to temple worship (as seen in the book of Psalms) binds this past age to our own. The chapter ends with words which reflect the earnestness of Jews living in the postexilic age: "We will not neglect the house of our God" (v. 39).

There were those in the postexilic community for whom the temple and its rituals were of secondary value (see, e.g., Mal. 1:6-8; 3:6-9). Quite likely, vv. 32-39 are to be seen as standing over against this attitude which discounts the importance of temple worship and service (cf. Neh. 13:10-11). Although, later on, temple worship will be superceded by the synagogue, at this time of history it still served as the center of Jewish life. Here, the people were bound not only to each other but also to God. In this holy place, Jews heard (through words and ritual) the saving history recounted and the commandments proclaimed. The temple gave voice to both "gospel and law."

THE PEOPLE OF JERUSALEM
AND JUDAH
Nehemiah 11:1-36

JERUSALEM: THE HOLY CITY (11:1-2)

In the book of Lamentations, we possess the sad reflections of
one who lived through or, at least, close to the time of Jerusalem's
destruction. The author of these laments remembers Jerusalem
as a beautiful, lively city, but the city he sees now before him is
a city of death. He cries out: "How lonely sits the city that was
full of people" (Lam. 1:1). Although, in the time of Ezra and
Nehemiah, the situation was much improved, still Jerusalem was
a city in need of people (Neh. 7:4). This situation is hard to
imagine because it was the city of David, the son of Yahweh; it
was the city that Yahweh had chosen as his dwelling place (Ps.
132:11-14; 76:2). The rebuilding of the Jerusalem temple after
the Exile was a reaffirmation of Jerusalem as the "dwelling place"
of Yahweh. However, many Jews preferred to live elsewhere. The
great Exilic Prophet, who depicted in colorful language the return
to the land and to Jerusalem (Isa. 52:1-2, 7-10), would have been
disappointed at the small number of Jews who chose to live in
the city which was so much the focus of his own hope.

The Will of God Discovered by Lot (11:1)

The relationship of chs. 11 – 13 to what precedes (and to each
other) is disputed. They appear to reflect various contexts and
time periods. For example, 11:1-2 seem to be a response to the
situation described in 7:4: "The city was wide and large, but the
people within it were few and no houses had been built." True,
many leaders of the people lived in this capital city (e.g., admin-
istrators such as Nehemiah and his staff; cf. 11:1), but the general
population avoided Jerusalem (because it was unsafe to live there?;
see 7:1-3). Since not enough people determined on their own to
live in Jerusalem, leaders in the restored community designed a

141

plan to repopulate the city: Lots were cast to determine the families that would relocate there. By this method one of every ten families would become citizens of Jerusalem. We are not given any information about how the people greeted this method of selection, but apparently the results derived by this traditional procedure were accepted as the will of God (cf. Prov. 16:33).

They Went Willingly (11:2)

Verse 2 speaks of those "who willingly offered to live in Jerusalem." This could refer to those who accepted the judgment of the lot with a gracious spirit, or it could refer to another group who took the initiative and volunteered to move to Jerusalem. In any case, those who moved "willingly" to this capital are "blessed" by their neighbors. This response may indicate that becoming a citizen of Jerusalem involved some hardship. The people moving to this city would hardly have been "blessed" if their relocation was actually a "move upward." Times of difficulty and need are often overcome because there are those in a community who are willing to bear extra responsibility so that the whole community may profit.

The Hebrew term underlying the words "who willingly offered" is *nadab* (see its use elsewhere, e.g., Exod. 25:2; 35:21, 29; 1 Chron. 29:5, 6). Another form of this same basic Hebrew root *(nedabah)* refers to an offering given to Yahweh. The RSV translates this term by "freewill offering" (e.g., Ps. 54:6). A freewill offering *(nedabah)* is that which one gives willingly. In Neh. 11:2 the people "who willingly offered" to move to Jerusalem became themselves something of a "freewill offering" because they "willingly offered" to live in Jerusalem.

In general, sacrifices are symbolic of what the offerer wishes to be in his relationship to God. Sacrifice and offering find their true fulfillment when one moves beyond sacrificing an animal and offers oneself. Paul speaks to this general principle in Rom. 12:1: "I appeal to you therefore, brethren . . . to present your bodies as a living sacrifice, holy and acceptable to God, which is your spiritual worship."

THESE ARE THE PEOPLE WHO LIVED IN JERUSALEM (11:3-24)

Although vv. 25-36 mention the fact that some Jews settled in other towns of the restored community, the greater part of the chapter is a listing of families that chose to live in Jerusalem.

Here, once more, we have a long list of names. The brief comments that accompany some of the names make us aware of the stature of many of those who took part in the resettling of Jerusalem. The "sons of Perez" were "valiant men" (*'anshe-hayil;* v. 6). They were not the only ones of such sturdy character, for among the priests were "mighty men of valor" (*gibbore-hayil;* v. 14). Without such people a community has little chance of a future.

A bit of sadness touches the heart, however, when one reads this list of names because time has swallowed them up; we know their names but no one is fully aware of their accomplishments or of the hardships under which they lived. But whoever has an appreciation for the difficult circumstances in which these people lived and worked will be thankful for their faithfulness to God. Although this list of names (as well as other similar lists in the Bible) is tedious to read, it underscores the truth that God's work on this earth is done by people.

Back Home Again, but Not Free (11:23-24)

With the arrival of the new settlers, the "holy city" was reborn. Once again Jerusalem's streets held the sound of people who blessed the name of Yahweh. It is a happy event, but vv. 23-24 are a reminder that despite the resettlement of Jerusalem, the Jews are not fully free; they still live under the rule of the Persian king. A representative of the Jewish community, Pethahiah, must report to the Persian ruler and be responsible for carrying out directives of the royal court. It is an honor of sorts, but his post is also a mark of humiliation; he represents a subjugated people.

Persian authority is evident even in the cult (see, e.g., the NEB, which gives the sense of v. 23: "For they were under the king's orders, and there was obligatory duty for the singers every day"). Jews may *worship* the God who created the world and celebrate his great power and authority, but, in actuality, the Persian king *controls* much of their life in the land. True, Jews have more freedom now than they had when they lived in exile, but they still suffer the pain of slavery (cf. 9:36-37). Although these texts do not record any explicit appeal to God for deliverance, one can well imagine (as mentioned in the last chapter) that such hope was alive in many Jewish hearts. Any kind of slavery constitutes in itself a cry for freedom.

PRIESTS AND LEVITES AND THE DEDICATION OF THE WALL
Nehemiah 12:1-47

PROMINENT PRIESTLY AND LEVITICAL FAMILIES (12:1-26)

The restored community in the land of Israel was created by laypersons and clergy who were willing to risk their future to establish a future for Israel. In these verses we have, once again, a listing of the names of priestly and Levitical families who belonged to this pioneering community. For a discussion of the dating of the list in 12:1-11 and its relationship to the listings in 12:12-21; 10:2-8; Ezra 2:36-39; and 1 Chron. 24:7-19, one may consult other commentaries.

A RETURN TO NEHEMIAH'S MEMOIRS (12:27-43)

Nehemiah's first-person account of events in the postexilic community was broken off at the end of ch. 7. Now, after the insertion of materials which are difficult to date (although chs. 8 – 9 probably come from the time of Ezra), the editor returns to the personal account of Nehemiah. With regard to Nehemiah's report, however, we are given no specific dates with which we can orient ourselves. Nevertheless, the reference to the dedication of the walls suggests that we should think of a time shortly after the completion of this building project (i.e., ca. 445 B.C.E.; cf. Neh. 6:15).

The Beginning and the End

Often, the end seems to be far distant from the beginning. Surely, it must have appeared so to the Jews who began to rebuild the walls around Jerusalem. According to Neh. 6:15, the rebuilding project was completed rather quickly — in fifty-two days. But the number of days or hours that it took to complete this project does not tell the whole story. This kind of time measurement says nothing of the pain and humiliation suffered by the Jews when Sanballat and Tobiah ridiculed them (4:1-3); it gives us no measure of the despair and anxiety that came upon them as they worked at this "impossible" task while, at the same time, remaining alert to fight off those opposed to their efforts (4:10-14).

Accept the Work of Our Hands

Finally, the wall is completed and the Jews offer to God the work of their hands. Their adversaries had thought that they could intimidate the Jewish workers so that "their hands will drop from the work, and it will not be done" (6:9), but commitment to Yahweh won out over fear of people (cf. Ps. 27:1; 56:4, 11).

In building this wall, these courageous Jews made a name for themselves, but not in the same way that the tower-builders in Gen. 11:1-9 attempted to do. Rather than trying to exalt themselves over against God, they established a reputation as "builders for God" (cf. the title of Lüthi's commentary, *Die Bauleute Gottes*). Their memory is associated with Jerusalem (not Babel), whose traditions have been transmitted far and wide to enrich the world. Having labored hard to complete their task, the Jews now dedicate the wall to God. The words of Ps. 90:17 could well have been theirs: "Let the favor of the Lord our God be upon us, and establish thou the work of our hands upon us, yea, the work of our hands establish thou it."

"With Gladness, with Thanksgivings" (12:27)

Success that follows hard work and struggle (such as the completion of the wall around Jerusalem) is especially sweet. Nehemiah's description of the dedication of the wall emphasizes the joy of this event (cf. esp. vv. 27, 40, 43). In v. 43, the word "rejoice" occurs five times (!), three times as a verb *(samah)* and twice as a noun *(simhah)*.

This joyous ceremony in which the city and its walls are dedicated to Yahweh stands in sharp contrast to the situation depicted in the book of Lamentations. There the author describes Jerusalem as a place of ruins, weeping, and despair; she is stunned by the devastation brought about by Yahweh (see, e.g., chs. 1 – 3). The book ends with a plea for restoration (Lam. 5:21). This prayer was heard. Yahweh, who once appeared as an enemy fighting against Jerusalem (Lam. 2:5), is now celebrated as the God who is with his people (Neh. 4:14-15) and who is determined to fight for them (Neh. 4:20). The city and its walls are rebuilt, and people, instead of jackals (Lam. 5:18), roam its streets. Once Jerusalem's humiliation and pain were known far and wide (Lam. 4:12, 15; Ezek. 26:2); now it is her joy that is "heard afar off" (Neh. 12:43; cf. Ezra 3:13).

Yahweh "dwells" once again in Jerusalem. Although Jerusalem does not actually have the name given it in Ezek. 48:35 ("Yahweh is there"), it is the sense of his presence among the Jews in the city that produces this happiness. Along with the singing and rejoicing at the dedication of the wall, there must have been also the hope that this was the beginning of Yahweh's new creation in which Jerusalem would be a center of joy and a city of peace (Isa. 65:17-25) — truly a city like the "Jerusalem above" (Gal. 4:26; Rev. 21:1-4).

A PEACEFUL COMMUNITY AT WORSHIP (12:44-47)

By the use of the phrase "on that day" (v. 44), the editor probably intends to connect this section with the day of dedication. The same wording occurs in 13:1, however, and there, as here, one can translate it "in that time" (so AV and JB). This rendering speaks of a longer time period which may include the day of dedication or a longer span of time. In any case, the author (probably not Nehemiah) gives us a summary of how the community functioned after the completion of the wall. It is an idyllic picture of the postexilic community in which laity and clergy perform faithfully the tasks assigned. All the clergy are represented as obeying the "command of David and his son Solomon" (v. 45). This comment is to be understood in the context of the tradition presented in 1 Chron. 23 – 26 and 2 Chron. 8:14 (but not in the books of Samuel or Kings). The passages in Chronicles portray David as the one who organized the priests, Levites, singers, and gatekeepers for service in the temple.

The View of the Insider (12:47)

The Jewish community, so we are informed, functioned in a peaceful and orderly manner "in the days of Zerubbabel and in the days of Nehemiah" (v. 47). This statement alerts us to the somewhat idealized nature of vv. 44-47. The author overlooked some of the conflicts that racked the community (e.g., Ezra 10:1-44; Neh. 6:18-19; 13:4-29). This account of the community is not that of the neutral observer; it derives from an "insider" — a "believer."

This kind of person "sees" more deeply into the community than the neutral observer. Certain actions of the community, to him, are prophetic of what the community really is (see, e.g., Neh. 10:28-39). The same kind of "prophetic seeing" (hyperbole) may be found in Acts 4:32-37.

EITHER — OR
Nehemiah 13:1-31

SEPARATION FROM FOREIGNERS (13:1-3)

The prophets speak often of Israel's disobedience, as do Ezra and Nehemiah. In fact, Israel's sinfulness is so often underscored in the Bible that we think, sometimes, that these ancient people were especially wicked. However, as today so then, it was most often the negative aspects of life that called for comment. In reference to the response of people to the will of God, the NT, like the OT, speaks more often of failure than of faithfulness.

This passage (vv. 1-3) does, however, speak of obedience and faithfulness: "On that day" the people listened to "the book of Moses" and *their listening became obedient action* (vv. 1, 3). On hearing the commandment from the Torah which prohibited the Ammonite and the Moabite from entering "the assembly *[qahal]* of God," the people "separated from Israel all those of foreign descent" (vv. 1, 3; cf. Deut. 23:3-5). The Hebrew word *qahal*, which is translated by "assembly" in Neh. 13:1 and Deut. 23:3, has the sense of a people gathered for cultic purposes. It may be, therefore, that while the foreigners were allowed to remain as part of the city population, they were not permitted to take part in cultic activities.

Doing More Than Is Demanded

David Clines ("Nehemiah 10," *JSOT* 21 [1981]: 116-17) has observed that "the spirit of the law can be more rigorous than the letter." One example of this truth may be found in the teaching of Jesus (Matt. 5:21-28). Another example is to be seen in Neh. 13:1-3. In Deut. 23:3-5, the law demands only that the Ammonites and the Moabites be barred from "the assembly of the LORD." But the leaders of the Jewish community during Nehemiah's time excluded not only those of Ammonite and Moabite ancestry, but "all those of foreign descent" (v. 3).

Did this blanket exclusion of foreigners apply to the Edomites and Egyptians as well? If so, then once again the people are asked to do more than is demanded and, in fact, are asked to do something contrary to the words of Torah. In the same Torah selection (Deut. 23:7-8), it is stated that "the children of the third generation that are born to them [i.e., to the Egyptians and Edomites] may enter the assembly of the LORD." Why did the Jewish community listen to the passage concerning the Ammonites and Moabites (Deut. 23:3-5) but let remain without comment the declaration concerning the Edomites and Egyptians (Deut. 23:7-8)? See our comments in the following paragraphs.

Scripture Interpretation Requires Good Sense

The Bible records various teachings that have arisen out of many different contexts. Some oracles, laws, and proverbs that "made sense" in one context *may* be appropriate for other contexts also, *but not* for every context. Thus a wise interpreter of Scripture is not one who merely understands the meaning of a certain biblical text; he is one who knows also *when* this passage applies to his situation or the situation of his community.

No doubt Deut. 23:3-6 was read to the community of Nehemiah's time because it was thought to be relevant to the issue of assimilation that threatened the vitality of the Jewish community. But the words preserved in Deut. 23:7-8 (regarding the Edomites and Egyptians) were not judged to be relevant. When people are struggling for survival and must deal with the problem of Jews assimilating with foreigners, should a text be read (i.e., Deut. 23:7-8) that seems to approve reception of foreigners into the community? With regard to this same issue (i.e., the relevance of certain scriptural passages), it may be noted that when Abraham is mentioned in Nehemiah, it is his "faithfulness" that is cited (Neh. 9:8); there is no emphasis on the promise made to Abraham: "By you all the families of the earth shall bless themselves" (Gen. 12:3). The latter emphasis was not "appropriate" to a people struggling for survival. For a similar reason, the book of Revelation makes no reference to teachings of non-resistance and honoring the emperor (see, e.g., Matt. 5:38-45; 1 Pet. 2:13-17).

On the Other Hand

Most people realize that no scripture applies to every situation, yet it may be important for us to ask *why* we listen to some texts and not to others. Perhaps, despite the risk, the Jewish community should have given a hearing to Deut. 23:7-8?! Sometimes we need to hear scripture that goes counter to our own day. In Jeremiah's time, the people thought that the scriptures centering on the David traditions were the relevant ones; but Jeremiah called them to hear the words of the Sinai covenant (Jer. 7 and 26). Further, in the history of the Church, people have sometimes decided too quickly that certain scriptural passages were irrelevant to the Church's life (e.g., texts that speak about social and political justice, or, perhaps, texts that call for personal piety). Sometimes the Church has felt threatened by these passages (as the Jewish community must have been threatened by Deut. 23:7-8); therefore it has been silent concerning them.

We must be careful not to trust too much to our "good sense" of what is relevant, because sometimes our "good sense" simply masks what *we* want. We even deceive ourselves with regard to the guidance of the Spirit of God. As we look back on history, we see (with the wisdom of hindsight) that some people who have claimed to be led by his Spirit in the interpretation of Scripture have merely urged their own likes and dislikes upon us (cf. Jer. 14:14-15).

THE REFORMER LEAVES; HIS OPPONENTS
EMERGE (13:4-9)

Eliashib and Tobiah

After guiding the restored community for twelve years, Nehemiah returns to Susa for a brief period. In his absence dissident elements assert themselves. Earlier chapters have made us aware that some powerful people in the Jewish community were not fully sympathetic to Nehemiah and his reform program. For example, a number of "the nobles" were friendly to Tobiah "the Ammonite" (6:10; cf. 2:10), an old enemy of Nehemiah (4:3). Although Tobiah has a good Hebrew name ("Yahweh is good") — possibly his mother was Jewish — he has set himself against Nehemiah's efforts to rebuild Jerusalem.

Tobiah is a sturdy opponent who is well established in the Jewish community: he is married to a Jew, as is his son (6:18), and he is "connected" (or is "close"; see Heb. *qarob*) to Eliashib the priest. This Eliashib may very well be the same person who is called the "high priest" in v. 28. It is possible that Tobiah was a relative of Eliashib because, at times, the Hebrew term *qarob* has this meaning (see, e.g., Ruth 2:20). In any case, it is clear that Tobiah has worked his way into the Jewish community;

through marriage relationships in the community he has developed strong family bonds and friendships.

The Risk of Intermarriage

Tobiah's family ties in the Jewish community illustrate the risk involved in intermarriage. People who move out of one religious, family background into another often carry with them some loyalty to the past life. As a member of a new family they exert significant influence on family life and worship. To a greater or lesser extent they will alter the religious traditions of the family and community. Unless these newcomers to the family take on the character of a Ruth (i.e., go through a conversion), their influence will tend to promote laxness in family and community religious traditions.

Even Eliashib the priest (probably the "high priest" mentioned in v. 28) allows his family relationship or friendship to Tobiah to dull his religious sensitivity. He permits Tobiah to take over a room in the temple precincts that had previously been set aside for the storage of cultic materials and objects (v. 5). For what purpose Tobiah used this room we are not told, but it was definitely set aside for his use. This wrong-headed and wrong-hearted decision of Eliashib was, no doubt, influenced by his "close" relationship to Tobiah. This action points up the difficulty Nehemiah had in bringing about change in the restored community. In addition to "outside" opposition, there were those among the Jews who did not want the Torah-true community advocated by Nehemiah. Nehemiah has inherited the pain of the prophets: the people (i.e., the priests) from whom he expects strong support turn out to be on the other side.

Nehemiah Is Angry

Nehemiah's anger over Tobiah's presence in the temple reminds one of the incident in which Jesus, with a whip, drove the money changers from the temple (John 2:14-18). Jesus, like Nehemiah, is thoroughly angered by those who mock God by using sacred space for personal use. Nehemiah "cleanses" the temple space (i.e., returns it to "cultic cleanness") and restores the room to its sacred service.

PROMISED SUPPORT IS WITHDRAWN (13:10-14)

The permission given to Tobiah to utilize temple space for his own purposes is only one example of carelessness regarding the temple. Verses 10-14 speak of another type of laxity. The "firm covenant" agreement recorded in 9:38 – 10:39 declared that the Levites are to receive the tithes (10:38). Apparently, it is this gift that supports the Levites in their sacred service (Num. 18:21). During Nehemiah's absence, however, this support of the Levites has been suspended. Nothing is said concerning the priests or the singers; apparently they continued to receive support.

The target of discrimination, as we have said, was the Levites. It may be that in these verses we are observing a power struggle of which we have hints elsewhere. In the book of Ezekiel, the Levites have a decidedly secondary role to play in the temple worship. They have this inferior status, so it is explained, because they went "astray" from Yahweh (Ezek. 44:10-14). This negative attitude toward the Levites, which some people had, may have influenced some of the Levites to remain in Babylon. Observe that Ezra had to send back messengers to persuade more Levites to join him in the journey to the land (Ezra 8:15-20). Why come back to the land, they must have thought, if they were not to be honored.

Whatever some people may have thought about the Levites, it is clear that Nehemiah valued them highly. How many others in the community shared his view we do not know. It seems certain that the leadership of the community (under the priests!) did not share Nehemiah's enthusiasm, for only Nehemiah's reappearance causes the tithe for the Levites to be reinstated.

Once again, in these verses, we may be witnessing the presence of opposing groups within the Jewish community. The opposition of "outsiders" to the community of faith would not be nearly so troubling if the community itself had oneness of heart. But, ironic as it may be, in communities which seek to serve and honor God, struggles for power are not infrequent.

THE SABBATH (13:15-22)

Profaning the Sabbath Brings God's Wrath (13:15-18)

It is not only Ezra and Nehemiah who are concerned about Sabbath observance; the Law and the prophets call upon Israel to keep the Sabbath (e.g., Exod. 20:8-11; 34:21; Deut. 5:12-15; Amos 8:5; Jer. 17:21; Ezek. 20:12-24). It was this disregard for the Sabbath that brought upon Israel the judgment of the Exile; God's wrath will come again upon the restored community if it continues to allow the buying and selling of goods on the Sabbath day (v. 18; cf. Jer. 17:27 and Ezek. 20:23-24). The threat which promises a judgment worse than the Exile on the Jews *if they do not keep the Sabbath* is a hyperbolic statment — an exaggeration. From the prophets we understand that the Exile came about for more basic reasons (see Jer. 7:1-15). The assumption is, no doubt, that people who have so little regard for the Sabbath probably are also lax with the so-called "weightier" matters of the Law.

Honoring the Sabbath

One should honor the Sabbath, so says a talmudic statement, because in so doing one honors the God who gave this holy day to humankind (B.T. *Yebamoth* 6a-6b). The refusal to honor God in this way means that such people will have little concern for God's teaching about how one should relate to other people. For example, see Amos's description of some people in his day; they rebel against observing the Sabbath because it "gets in the way." They can hardly wait for the Sabbath to be over so that they can get on with what is important to them, namely, taking advantage of the poor and making profit for themselves (Amos 8:4-6).

Some people in the time of Nehemiah have similar thoughts. They cannot control their covetous nature even for one day; they simply must increase their profits. Abraham Heschel's comments on the observance of the Sabbath would have pleased the prophets and Nehemiah (*Between God and Man,* ed. F. Rothschild, 227):

> Judaism tries to foster the vision of life as a pilgrimage to the seventh day. . . . It seeks to displace the coveting of things in space for *coveting the things in time,* teaching man to covet the seventh day all days of the week. God himself coveted that day, He called it *Hemdat Yamim,* a day to be coveted. It is as if the command: *Do not covet things of space,* were correlated with the unspoken word: *Do covet things of time.*

Although Jesus was angry at some Pharisees who would not permit some good acts to be done on the Sabbath (Mark 3:1-6), it is likely that he would have been one with Amos and Nehemiah in their attempt to keep the Sabbath holy.

Sometimes a Show of Force Is Necessary (13:19-22)

It is never pleasant to observe an angry person, but one cannot always be pleasant in relating to people. In some confrontations in which people exhibit hard-core opposition to that which is holy and good, anger may be the appropriate response. In his day, Jesus expressed such anger (cf. Mark 3:1-6 and John 2:13-16).

153

Nehemiah became angry also at those whose actions stood over against Torah and the *shalom* of the community. In opposing Tobiah's personal use of a room in the temple precincts, Nehemiah was concerned about honoring *holy space;* in his anger against those who wanted to make the Sabbath just another day of buying and selling, he wanted to protect *holy time.* In the Jewish and Christian traditions, holy space and time protect the holiness and humaneness of life. A society which has no regard for the holiness of space and time could easily become a society which has little regard for other persons outside one's own family and circle of friends.

Nehemiah's threat of force was enough to stop (for a time at least) the blatant disregard for the Sabbath. Naturally, one cannot compel others to be moral or humane, but sometimes the threat of or the use of force may stop some people from ruining life for others. Further, such action at times encourages other people to take a stand against those who offend and ruin community traditions.

INTERMARRIAGE IN THE GENERAL POPULATION (13:23-27)

Intermarriage will always constitute a central problem for close-knit, separatistic communities. This problem is one that has surfaced several times already in the books of Ezra and Nehemiah (e.g., Ezra 9 – 10; Neh. 6:18; 10:30). See our commentary on these passages.

Knowing Hebrew; Understanding Torah

The text of vv. 23-27 is somewhat ambiguous, but the main point of the narrative is not in doubt: children who are raised in mixed marriages are frequently unable to speak Hebrew. The non-Jewish mothers, who are in charge of the children's education, do not speak Hebrew themselves; therefore the children fail to learn the language of their ancestors.

This inability to speak the language sets the children at a distance from the teachings of Torah. Such a situation is unacceptable to a community that treasures Torah as the way of life, because Torah will not continue to be the center of the community if an increasing number of children are growing up without full knowledge of Hebrew. True, the Jewish community may still survive, even with continued intermarriage, *but there is a big difference between a community that survives and a community that lives.*

Nehemiah: "I Accuse"

Israel's future is threatened by intermarriage; Nehemiah "contended" (from *rib*) with those involved, that is, he brought public charges against them (see the occurrence of Heb. *rib* in 5:7; 13:11, 17). The charge is forcefully made with a curse (from *qalal*). Nehemiah is not a "democratic" person who assumes that everything can be discussed. He is persuaded that intermarriage violates the teaching of Torah and is ruinous of the community; therefore he sets himself fully against the people who enter into such marriages. Filled with rage, he beats and curses the offenders (v. 25) — not unusual actions for people of his time and place in history (nor of people in some present-day communities).

The pain of seeing many children of intermarriage unable to speak Hebrew (vv. 23-25) tore at the heart of Nehemiah. These marriages threatened the future of the Jewish community, so Nehemiah believed, because often the children of these marriages are on the periphery of this covenant community. These verses remind one of the story of Esau, who "despised his birthright" (Gen. 25:34) and sold it to Jacob. Nehemiah is attempting to halt intermarriage because, among other things, he believes that Jews involved in such marriages are selling the birthright of the children born in this marriage bond. What is this birthright? It is a chance to live in a Jewish home where one's life is guided by Torah — God's gift to every Jew. For an extended discussion of intermarriage, see our comments on Ezra 9 – 10.

With Curses and Physical Abuse (13:25)

Nehemiah is not alone in his violence, as we have emphasized above. For example, the anger of Jesus was not simply "spiritual" anger; it was real anger (Mark 3:1-6) which sometimes involved inflamed speech (e.g., Matt. 18:1-6; 23:1-39; cf. Gal. 5:12; Rev. 16) as well as physical violence (John 2:15). The anger expressed by Jesus, Paul, John, the author of the book of Revelation (against Rome), or Nehemiah is *not simply the rage of a "hothead"* (although that was the accusation made against Nehemiah in B.T. *Sanhedrin* 93b); *it is intentional anger,* an anger that is aroused by concern for the relation of the individual and community to God.

Anger is powerful and dangerous; it can so easily destroy. But a passive piety has often allowed wrongful practices to take place against the weak, the poor, and minority people. We guard our own "personal" piety while allowing evil to ruin others. Sometimes we speak of developing a "God-like" or (for Christians) a

155

"Christ-like" character. Often, the image suggested by these descriptions is of a pious, nice person. We forget that the God of the Bible is stirred, at times, to great anger. It is an anger that the prophets share as they look out on people in the Israelite community who do not care for the teaching of Torah (see, e.g., Amos 8). Although we may not wish to adopt today the practices of Nehemiah (or of Jesus in his use of a whip in cleansing the temple?), his actions remind us that, at times, a leader must take assertive, forceful action to restrain destructive people.

INTERMARRIAGE AT THE TOP (13:28-31)

A Priest Marries an Outsider

Intermarriage always poses dangers to a close-knit, religious community, but it becomes especially threatening when it concerns influential people. Nehemiah is outraged to learn that a young man (a priest) from the family of the high priest has married the daughter of Nehemiah's determined foe, Sanballat. Nehemiah will not let this nervy challenge to his reform program pass without response. He takes action even though he is dealing with a family that holds considerable power in the community. Like the prophets, he does not back away from powerful people.

The Law recognized the obvious dangers in intermarriage when it commanded that the high priest must marry a woman from Israel (Lev. 21:14). It simply would not do to have a foreign woman teaching the children of the high priest! But for every male member of the high priest's family, there existed the possiblity of becoming the high priest; therefore, "good Torah sense" decreed that any intermarriage involving family members would be a serious breach of Torah faith. Further, this case of intermarriage, which involves the priest's family with that of Sanballat (who opposes Nehemiah), would be an outright challenge to Nehemiah's leadership.

Nehemiah sees the danger in this marriage: what Sanballat could not achieve by his public attacks on Nehemiah and his program he may now accomplish through his son-in-law. Although a later, more permissive, democratic society may wish to honor a couple who would break out of a restrictive, separatistic structure, Nehemiah (looking at life from his time and place) views it as a tragedy and calls upon God to remember the family that has allowed this marriage to take place.

Nehemiah declares, "I chased him from me" (v. 28). He would

not allow this priest to continue in his holy office; he forced him
to leave the community. But Nehemiah did not limit his action
to the individual priest. He declares that he "cleansed" the priests
from everything foreign. Further, he "established the duties of the
priests and Levites" (v. 30). We do not know what happened in
detail. It is only a summary of a conflict; its resolution may have
taken a long period of time. But, as we know, it was not a final
resolution. The issue of how a religious community should relate
to the world "outside" — especially in terms of intimate relationships — continues to be a matter of concern.

REMEMBER THEM (13:29)

On another occasion, Nehemiah has called upon God to "remember" those outside of the community who have opposed him (e.g.,
6:14; cf. 4:3-5). The burden of their continual opposition was
heavy; however, more painful than the outside obstructionism
was the rebellion of the "insiders." Prophets and prophetesses,
people on whom he thought he could rely, cooperated with Tobiah
and Sanballat in opposing him (6:14). Nehemiah had no sure
support among the priests either. In the present passage, he calls
upon God to judge these priests who have violated the "spirit"
if not the "letter" of Torah. They have defiled the Torah of which
they are interpreters and therefore have "defiled the priesthood"
(cf. Mal. 2:7-9).

It is the old, old story: Nehemiah may not be identified as a
prophet, but, like the prophet, he knows what it is to stand over
against prophets and priests who have pulled away from the path
of Torah (see Hos. 4:4-6). Finally, Nehemiah exerts his authority
and banishes the priest (the son-in-law of Sanballat) from the
community. It is not a pleasant act, but if Nehemiah is to preserve
his integrity and that of Torah, it is an action that "finally" had
to be taken.

REMEMBER ME (13:31)

Nehemiah and the Psalms of Lament

This prayer, which is repeated three times in ch. 13 (vv. 14, 22,
31), *appears to be an inappropriate* plea to God. It is so bold; the one
who prays these words could be accused of self-righteousness (as
he was in B.T. *Sanhedrin* 93b). Although this exact kind of petition
is unusual, it is not foreign to Israelite thought. For example, the
thought underlying the protestation of innocence in some of the

157

Psalms is the belief that the worshiper has lived in a way that should call forth blessing (i.e., remembrance) from God. When, instead, he experiences pain, opposition, or sickness, he believes that he has been treated unfairly (see, e.g., Pss. 17 and 26; see also Jer. 18:20).

Nehemiah: Not Self-Righteous

Whatever the background to the petition "remember me," it sounds bad. Are we not just sinners, saved by grace? After having done all that we have done for God, must we not simply say that we are slaves and have done no more than what was expected of us (cf. Luke 17:7-10)? This hard word needs to be heard on occasion because the tendency to pride and self-righteousness is always with us. With regard to Nehemiah, however, another view seems closer to the truth. His plea to be remembered by God is a cry of pain. Like Jeremiah (cf. Jer. 18:20), he stands alone in leadership as a spokesman for Torah. Notice that when he leaves the community for a period of time, the reform fails (Neh. 13:20). He is a strong leader among the returned Jews; the burden of this kind of leadership often brings depression and anxiety (see the case of Elijah in 1 Kgs. 19:4). Receiving little support in the community, he crys out to God: "Remember me."

Is God Ever Pleased with Us?

Does God, like his servant Paul, "appreciate" what people do for him (cf. Rom. 16:1-4)? God takes notice of us, declare some biblical writers; he finds pleasure in our devotion (cf. Neh. 13:14). The author of 1 Pet. 2:20 encourages the Christians of his day by observing: "When you have behaved well and suffer for it, your fortitude is a fine thing in the sight of God" (NEB). Paul fights the "good fight," finishes the race, and holds to the faith (2 Tim. 4:7). He believes that God likes what he has done and that he will receive a reward for it (2 Tim. 4:8). Hebrews 6:10 announces that God was pleased with Enoch. Sometimes we stress the sinfulness of humankind so much that it appears we can never please God. There are people who are never pleased with what others do, but God is not like that. He is pleased with the faithful servant (Matt. 25:21).

Life has moved on since the time of Nehemiah; we would not care to "go back" to his time or to his specific programs. He may not always have been right, but in his heart he bore concern for God's teaching, and one can believe that, for this, God does remember him.

BIBLIOGRAPHY OF WORKS CITED

Books

Achtemeier, E. R. *The Community and Message of Isaiah 56 – 66: A Theological Commentary* (Minneapolis: Augsburg, 1982).

Ackroyd, P. R. *I & II Chronicles, Ezra, Nehemiah*. Torch Bible Commentary (London: SCM, 1973).

Agus, J. *The Evolution of Jewish Thought* (New York: Abelard and Schuman, 1959).

Berkovits, E. *Not in Heaven: The Nature and Function of Halakha* (New York: KTAV, 1983).

Bickerman, E. *From Ezra to the Last of the Maccabees* (New York: Schocken, 1962).

Blackman, P., ed. and trans. *Mishnayoth*. Vol. 2: *Pesahim* (New York: Judaica Press, 1963-64).

Bright, J. *A History of Israel*. 3rd ed. (Philadelphia: Westminster, 1981).

Buber, M. *On the Bible*. Ed. N. N. Glatzer (New York: Schocken, 1968).

Carroll, R. P. *When Prophecy Failed: Cognitive Dissonance in the Prophetic Traditions of the Old Testament* (London: SCM; New York: Seabury, 1979).

Clines, D. J. E. *Ezra, Nehemiah, Esther*. New Century Bible Commentary (London: Marshall, Morgan & Scott; Grand Rapids: Eerdmans, 1984).

Coggins, R. J. *The Books of Ezra and Nehemiah*. Cambridge Bible Commentary on the New English Bible (Cambridge: Cambridge University Press, 1976).

Daly, R. J. *The Origins of the Christian Doctrine of Sacrifice* (Philadelphia: Fortress, 1978).

De Vaux, R. *Ancient Israel: Its Life and Institutions*. Trans. J. McHugh (New York: McGraw-Hill, 1961; repr. 1965).

Ellison, H. L. *From Babylon to Bethlehem* (Exeter: Paternoster, 1976).

Fensham, F. C. *The Books of Ezra and Nehemiah.* New International Commentary on the Old Testament (Grand Rapids: Eerdmans, 1982).

Hamlin, E. J. *Inheriting the Land: Joshua.* International Theological Commentary (Grand Rapids: Eerdmans, 1983).

Hanson, P. *The Dawn of Apocalyptic: The Historical and Sociological Roots of Jewish Apocalyptic Eschatology.* 2nd ed. (Philadelphia: Fortress, 1979).

Heschel, A. J. *Man Is Not Alone: A Philosophy of Religion* (New York: Farrar, Straus and Giroux, 1951).

_____. *Between God and Man: An Interpretation of Judaism.* Ed. F. A. Rothschild (New York: Harper & Brothers, 1959).

Holmgren, F. C. *The God Who Cares: A Christian Looks at Judaism* (Atlanta: John Knox, 1979).

Jagersma, H. *A History of Israel in the Old Testament Period.* Trans. J. Bowden (London: SCM; Philadelphia: Fortress, 1983).

Kaufmann, Y. *History of the Religion of Israel.* Vol. 4: *From the Babylonian Captivity to the End of Prophecy.* Trans. C. W. Efroymson (New York: KTAV, 1977).

Kellermann, U. *Nehemia: Quellen, Überlieferung und Geschichte.* Beihefte zur Zeitschrift für die alttestamentliche Wissenschaft 102 (Berlin: A. Töpelmann, 1967).

Kidner, D. *Ezra and Nehemiah.* Tyndale Old Testament Commentary (Leicester and Downers Grove, IL: Inter-Varsity, 1979).

Knight, G. A. F. *The New Israel: Isaiah 56 – 66.* International Theological Commentary (Grand Rapids: Eerdmans, 1985).

Kraft, C. H. *Christianity in Culture: A Study in Dynamic Biblical Theologizing in Cross-cultural Perspective* (Maryknoll, NY: Orbis, 1979).

Le Déaut, R. *La Nuit Pascale* (Rome: Pontifical Biblical Institute, 1963).

Lüthi, W. *Die Bauleute Gottes* (Basel: F. Reinhardt, 1945).

Marmur, D. *Intermarriage* (London: Reform Synagogues of Great Britain, 1978).

Mbiti, J. S. *African Religions and Philosophy* (Garden City, NY: Doubleday, 1970).

Myers, J. M. *Ezra. Nehemiah.* Anchor Bible (Garden City, NY: Doubleday, 1965).

Nickelsburg, G., and M. Stone. *Faith and Piety in Early Judaism: Texts and Documents* (Philadelphia: Fortress, 1983).

Pritchard, J. B., ed. *Ancient Near Eastern Texts Relating to the Old Testament.* 3rd ed. (Princeton: Princeton University Press, 1969).

Rabinowitz, Y. *The Book of Ezra*. ArtScroll Tanach Series (Brooklyn: Mesorah Publications, 1984).

Ringgren, H. *Sacrifice in the Bible* (New York: Association, 1962).

Ryle, H. E. *The Books of Ezra and Nehemiah*. Cambridge Bible for Schools and Colleges (Cambridge: Cambridge University Press, 1897).

Silver, D. J. *A History of Judaism*. Vol. 1: *From Abraham to Maimonides* (New York: Basic Books, 1974).

Stuhlmueller, C. *Haggai and Zechariah*. International Theological Commentary (Grand Rapids: Eerdmans, forthcoming).

Terrien, S. *The Elusive Presence: Toward a New Biblical Theology* (San Francisco: Harper & Row, 1978).

Von Rad, G. *Studies in Deuteronomy*. Trans. D. M. G. Stalker. Studies in Biblical Theology 1/9 (London: SCM; Chicago: H. Regnery, 1953).

Williamson, H. G. M. *Ezra, Nehemiah*. Word Biblical Commentary (Waco, TX: Word, 1985).

Articles

Andrews, D. K. "Yahweh the God of the Heavens." In *The Seed of Wisdom*. Festschrift for T. J. Meek. Ed. W. S. McCullough (Toronto: Toronto University Press, 1964), 45-57.

Carroll, R. P. "Twilight of Prophecy or Dawn of Apocalyptic?" *Journal for the Study of the Old Testament* 14 (1979): 3-35.

Clines, D. J. .A. "Nehemiah 10 as an Example of Early Jewish Biblical Exegesis," *Journal for the Study of the Old Testament* 21 (1981): 111-17.

Coggins, R. J. "The Interpretation of Ezra 4:4," *Journal of Theological Studies* 16 (1965): 124-27.

Füglister, N. "Passover." In *Sacramentum Mundi: An Encyclopedia of Theology*. Ed. K. Rahner et al. (New York: Herder and Herder, 1969) 4:352-57.

Galling, K. "The 'Gola List' according to Ezra 2 // Nehemiah 7," (trans. C. R. Simon) *Journal of Biblical Literature* 70 (1951): 149-58.

Holmgren, F. C. "A New Covenant? For Whom?" *The Ecumenist* 22 (1984): 38-41.

Japhet, S. "The Supposed Common Authorship of Chronicles and Ezra-Nehemiah Investigated Anew," *Vetus Testamentum* 18 (1968): 330-71.

Koch, K. "Ezra and the Origins of Judaism," *Journal of Semitic Studies* 19 (1974): 173-97.

Kuhrt, A. "The Cyrus Cylinder and Achaemenid Imperial Policy," *Journal for the Study of the Old Testament* 25 (1983): 83-97.

Martin, V. "Marriage et Famille dan les Groupes Christianises ou en voie de Christianisation de Dakar." In *Christianity in Tropical Africa.* Ed. C. G. Baeta (London: Oxford University Press, 1968), 362-95.

Myers, J. M. "Scribe." In *Interpreter's Dictionary of the Bible.* Ed. G. A. Buttrick et al. (New York: Abingdon, 1962) 4:246-48.

Peterson, D. "Zerubbabel and Jerusalem Temple Reconstruction," *Catholic Biblical Quarterly* 36 (1974): 366-72.

Runnalls, D. "The King as Temple Builder: A Messianic Typology." In *Spirit Within Structure.* Festschrift for G. Johnston. Ed. E. J. Furcha. Pittsburgh Theological Monograph Series 3 (Allison Park, Pa.: Pickwick, 1983), 15-37.

Schultz, C. "The Political Tensions Reflected in Ezra-Nehemiah." In *Scripture in Context.* Ed. C. D. Evans et al. (Pittsburgh: Pickwick, 1980), 221-44.

Widengren, G. "The Persian Period." In *Israelite and Judean History.* Old Testament Library. Ed. J. Hayes and J. Miller (London: SCM; Philadelphia: Westminster, 1977), 489-538.